THE JEWISH QUARTERLY

The Jewish Quarterly is published four times a year
by The Jewish Quarterly Pty Ltd

Publisher: Morry Schwartz

ISBN 9781760645397 E-ISBN 9781743823798
ISSN 0449010X E-ISSN 23262516

ALL RIGHTS RESERVED.
No part of this publication may be reproduced, stored in a retrieval system or transmitted in any form by any means electronic, mechanical, photocopying, recording or otherwise without the prior consent of the publishers.

Essay © retained by the author

Subscriptions 1 year print & digital (4 issues): £55 GBP | $75 USD.
1 year digital only: £35 GBP | $45 USD. Payment may be made by Mastercard or Visa. Payment includes postage and handling.

Subscribe online at jewishquarterly.com or email subscribe@jewishquarterly.com
Correspondence should be addressed to: The Editor, The Jewish Quarterly,
22–24 Northumberland Street, Collingwood VIC 3066 Australia
Phone +61 3 9486 0288 Email enquiries@jewishquarterly.com

The Jewish Quarterly is published under licence from the
Jewish Literary Trust Limited, which exercises a governance function.

UK Company Number: 01189861. UK Charity Commission Number: 268589.

Directors of the Jewish Literary Trust: Michael Mocatta (co-chair), Andrew Renton (co-chair), Lance Blackstone (chair emeritus), Devorah Baum, Phillip Blumberg, Ian Buruma, John Cohen, Shelly Freeman, Larraine Solomons, Michael Strelitz.

Founding Editor: Jacob Sonntag.

Editor: Jonathan Pearlman. Associate Editors: Jo Rosenberg and Emma Schwarcz. Management: Elisabeth Young. Publishing Manager: Becky Litwin. Marketing & Subscriptions Coordinator: Chloe Sloman. Design: John Warwicker and Tristan Main. Production: Marilyn de Castro. Typesetting: Tristan Main.

Printed and bound in the UK by Bell & Bain Ltd, Glasgow. The paper used to produce this book comes from wood grown in sustainable forests.

Issue 257, August 2024

THE JEWISH QUARTERLY

Whitewash

Poland and the Jews

Jan Grabowski is a Polish-Canadian professor of history at the University of Ottawa. His books include *Hunt for the Jews*, *Night Without End* and *On Duty: The Role of the Polish Blue and Criminal Police in the Holocaust*.

This edition of The Jewish Quarterly is proudly sponsored by the Anglo-Jewish Association. The AJA has been a passionate supporter of Jewish culture and Jewish interests since 1871.

https://www.anglojewish.org.uk

Whitewash

Poland and the Jews

Jan Grabowski

> *The notion of a usable past is key: In order to fortify national consciousness, and therefore the nationalist political leadership, a past has to be found that can be used to educate – more precisely, to indoctrinate – the nation, young and old. When such an uplifting past is unavailable, it has to be invented.*
> —Yehuda Bauer, 2020

On the evening of 30 May 2023, I strolled along Ujazdowskie Avenue, in a prestigious Warsaw neighbourhood, towards the neoclassicist building housing the German Historical Institute, where I was to deliver a lecture titled "The Polish (growing) problem with the Holocaust". In front of the institute I saw two police vans, lights flashing, with several officers and a growing number of agitated people congregating around the entrance. On my way in, I noticed hostile stares and overheard obscenities shouted in my direction. If I were a politician, or a media personality, the scene might somehow have made sense. But for a researcher, and a historian, whose publications were usually absorbed by a small circle of academic colleagues, all of this was very unusual.

The demonstrators, as I learned, had been mobilised by Robert Bąkiewicz, a right-wing extremist, a candidate for the parliament and darling of the Polish authorities, well funded by the state. In front of me, protesters (some of them with children in tow), held banners which read: "German crimes, German responsibility!", "Poles were the victims" and "Germans murdered six million Poles". This last poster would have come as a surprise to the 3 million murdered Polish Jews who, posthumously and unceremoniously, have been recruited to the cause of Polish martyrdom with which they had little, or nothing, to do. It echoed the recently revealed email exchange between the then Polish PM Mateusz Morawiecki and his friend, right-wing publicist Bronisław Wildstein, in which Wildstein suggested, that "Polish martyrdom should be promoted with the help of Jewish martyrdom – and it's possible". The protesters were proof that, indeed, it *was* possible.

Some of the banners and posters were in German, as if to reveal the face of the enemy lurking inside the building. Across the street I saw a van from the ubiquitous TVP, the Polish state-owned TV station, which, after the nationalist electoral victory in Poland in 2015, became an unapologetic centre of primitive and pervasive pro-government propaganda.

Inside the German Historical Institute, in the lecture room, the atmosphere was tense. Seated in the front row, glaring at me, was Grzegorz Braun, a member of the Polish Parliament (Sejm) and a militant antisemite, with his entourage. Further back, I saw several other nationalists, employees of the Institute of National Remembrance, a state institution charged with the enforcement of the official "party line" in matters of history. I knew that this crowd was not here to discuss history but to confront me, and to vent their anger at the "anti-Polish lies and conspiracy", as the government propaganda refers to the work of historians trying to shed light on the more controversial parts of the national past. Nevertheless, while I was prepared for a hostile Q&A session, I was not ready for the physical confrontation and violence which ensued.

> *Finally, the police made their appearance. And did nothing*

I had barely finished the introduction when Braun jumped to his feet, crossed the floor, grabbed the heavy microphone from the stand and – shouting, "Enough!" – started to smash it on the podium, right in front of me. A moment later, dropping what remained of the microphone, he rushed towards the loudspeakers and threw them to the ground, ripping out the electrical cords as he moved around the room. Mayhem erupted; the lecture was over. Students who came to hear the talk, some of them visibly traumatised and crying, started to shout (pointing at Braun): "Shame! Shame!" Close to me, one of the journalists who'd arrived with the Polish parliamentarian, hissed, "Jewish lies!" Finally, the police made their appearance. And did nothing. In 2023, doing nothing in the face of violence perpetrated by nationalists and right-wing extremists had become a behavioural pattern for the agents of the Polish state.

The sight of a raging extremist politician, flanked by immobile police, will be one of the enduring impressions of that evening. Another impression, much more important, was the realisation that scholars of the Holocaust were no longer victims only of verbal campaigns of hate orchestrated by the authorities. In Poland, today, words of hate have mutated into acts of physical violence directed against those who refuse to follow the official, state-approved historical narrative. The 1930s meet the 2020s. One hundred years of lessons unlearned and forgotten.

Professor Irena Grudzińska-Gross, in a poignant essay on the Democracy Seminar website, described the affair in the following words:

On May 30, in Warsaw, the Polish Sejm MP Grzegorz Braun interrupted a lecture by Professor Jan Grabowski, a historian reporting on the state of research about the World War II extinction of Polish Jews. Braun climbed onto the rostrum, threatening Grabowski, and trashed the microphone and speakers – as if not only physically, but also symbolically taking away the lecturer's voice. Since there are no longer any groupings of recognizable Jews in Poland, the assault on Jan Grabowski is the symbolic equivalent of a pogrom. The otherwise inexplicable destruction of property forms part of the pogrom repertoire.

To tell the truth, I should not have been surprised. Two weeks before the lecture, *Tygodnik Powszechny* – a well-respected, mainstream, Catholic and liberal (which, in Poland, rarely go together) weekly magazine – reported that my findings and methodology were flawed, and "the effects of my work were lamentable" (*skutki są opłakane*). What deputy-editor-in-chief Michał Okoński found "lamentable" were my estimates of Jewish losses at the hands of the Poles during the Holocaust, which I have established at around 200,000 victims. This number includes Jews who perished with direct or indirect involvement of their gentile neighbours. To make matters worse, Okoński attacked me while defending other Polish Holocaust scholars (who did not subscribe to my estimates) targeted by the hate campaign initiated by Polish authorities. The message was clear: here are our historians, who deserve support and whom we will defend. But in his case, Okoński winked at the authorities, gesturing at me – you are free to act.

Next was Jakub Kumoch, former adviser to the Polish president and now Polish ambassador to China, a popular figure among Polish right-wing extremists and radicals, who drew hostile attention to my upcoming lecture on social media. On state TV and radio and in the government-aligned press the hysteria was brewing. "German lackey", "He lies about Poland and Poles", "Falsifier of our past", I read about myself in the media. Michał Sopiński, chancellor and provost of Akademia Wymiaru Sprawiedliwości, a judicial academy in Warsaw, shared his thoughts on Twitter: "Take away his professorial title. Take away his citizenship. At least we don't have to shave his head because this disgusting liar Grabowski is already bald!" This I could understand: I could hardly expect anything else from the state-owned media and the state-owned people. But the earlier attack by Okoński and *Tygodnik Powszechny* left me perplexed, upset and worried.

So what was it that Braun prevented me from saying? In short, I wanted to argue that, however surprising it may sound, the question of Polish complicity in the Holocaust has become more contentious and divisive the further we are removed from the event. That the history of the Shoah in today's Poland is being corroded by the toxic mix of government policies of negationism and distortion willingly accepted by the broader public. That Poland has become a champion (worldwide) of Holocaust relativisation, Holocaust de-judaisation and Holocaust envy, insisting on Jewish–Bolshevik collusion and conspiracy, and blaming the victims for their own demise. Finally, I wanted to talk about the success of these memorial policies, which, over the years, have transformed how Poles see their own past and how they construe their own identity.

> *The politics of memory enforced in Poland are nowadays best described as Holocaust distortion*

Why Poland?

Why is the Polish case so vital to the memory of the Shoah? First, Poland is the place where the Holocaust was perpetrated; it's here, on pre-war Polish territory, that close to 5 out of 6 million Jews were put to death. The Jewish community in Poland was the largest in Europe, and second largest in the world, after the United States. Second, out of 3 million Polish Jews who – at some point – found themselves under German occupation, fewer than 30,000 survived the war. The survival rate for Polish Jews was, therefore, close to 1 per cent. Nowhere else in Europe was the Holocaust so complete, so total; nowhere else did the destruction of the Jewish people proceed with such nightmarish perfection. Third, Poland is where the Germans established all the extermination camps: Auschwitz, Treblinka, Chełmno, Sobibor, Majdanek and Bełżec. This, in turn, imposed on Polish society and the Polish state a unique obligation of memory, a duty of caring for the spaces of horror and for the symbolic commemoration of one of the greatest human catastrophes in history. That's why Poland, despite itself, has become a reluctant custodian of the memory of the Shoah.

These three reasons alone are enough to make us consider Poland, in matters of memory and commemoration of the Shoah, a place of unique importance. Unfortunately, the politics of memory pursued and enforced in Poland are nowadays best described as Holocaust distortion. Unlike Holocaust deniers of yesteryear, states, institutions and people engaged in Holocaust distortion do not deny the factuality of the Jewish catastrophe. They freely admit that the Germans murdered 6 million European Jews. What they refuse to acknowledge, however, is that their people, their nation, had something to do with the event. That their ancestors took part in the German genocidal project.

Holocaust distortion (or negationism) is a particularly insidious threat to our collective memory, as it is partially based on truth: no one denies, for instance, that some gentiles helped the Jews. The negationists insist, though, that helping Jews was the default position of their nation. They claim that Polish (or Hungarian, or Lithuanian, or Romanian, or Ukrainian) society did all it could to save its Jewish co-citizens in their moment of need. Israeli author Manfred Gerstenfeld called this memorial strategy "Holocaust deflection":

> [I]t entails admitting that the Holocaust happened while denying the complicity or responsibilities of specific groups or individuals. The Holocaust is then blamed on others. This, to a large extent, concerns those countries where, during the war, Germans were helped greatly by local citizens in the despoliation, deportation and killing of the Jews.

In practical terms, in Poland, it means shifting the entire blame to the Germans, regardless of the level of complicity of local gentiles. It was best summed up by the Polish writer and historian Kazimierz Wyka, who, shortly after the war, referring to the massive amount of Jewish real estate left in the hands of the Poles, wrote: "For the Germans, all the blame. For us – the keys and the cash."

In terms of advancing Holocaust distortion, Poland is ahead of the pack, but it is not alone. In Budapest, the local authorities erected, in 2014, a monument called the Memorial for Victims of the German Occupation. The Memorial of Hungarian Innocence would be a more appropriate name for the structure, which features Archangel Gabriel (patron saint of Hungary) attacked from above by a German eagle. The eagle has the date "1944" etched on its ankle. The message the monument wants to convey is simple: it was the Germans, and not us, who delivered, in 1944, 430,000 Hungarian Jews to the gas chambers in Auschwitz. This claim is a bald-faced lie. True, Adolph Eichmann and his people ordered the deportations, but the planning, the concentration of Jews in the ghettos, the robbery of their property and their subsequent transportation to the border with the *Generalgouvernement*, was prepared and executed by Hungarian civil authorities, police and the military.

In Lithuania, Ukraine and Latvia, dozens of anti-communist and patriotic fighters are now hailed as national heroes – including Jonas Noreika, Kazys Škirpa and Antanas Baltūsis-Žvejys in Lithuania, Stepan Bandera and Roman Shukhevych in Ukraine, and Herberts Cukurs in Latvia – despite ample evidence of their involvement with the Einsatzgruppen, the German mobile killing units responsible for thousands of Jewish deaths. In Bulgaria, the official historical narrative paints the country as a safe haven for Jews, conveniently forgetting the more than 11,000 Jews deported, in March 1943, by Bulgarian military authorities, from Macedonia and Thrace to Treblinka. The list goes on. Deflecting and distorting the history of the Holocaust allows governments today to construct a new, positive and *usable* narrative.

People and institutions engaging in Holocaust distortion tend to spotlight the Jewish police or the role played by the Jewish councils (Judenräte), inflating the scale of Jewish complicity. We will soon revisit this issue. Stressing the importance of the alleged Jewish collaboration with the communists is another technique often used by Holocaust distortionists. "The Jews had it coming," they claim, discussing the wave of anti-Jewish violence and pogroms in Eastern Europe, which started in the summer and autumn of 1941, after the German attack against the Soviet Union. This assertion not only relies on antisemitic stereotypes but also overlooks the reality that Jews were targeted irrespective of their political beliefs, and the perpetrators were drawn from diverse strata of society, including even those who earlier cooperated with the communists. Last, the negationists strive to elevate the wartime suffering of their own national group to the desired "Jewish" level, a phenomenon known as Holocaust envy. All of these symptoms of Holocaust distortion and denial will be at the heart of this essay.

> *The negationists strive to elevate the wartime suffering of their own national group to the desired "Jewish" level*

Enforcing the lies

From the beginning of this century the politics of memory started to play a prominent role in Poland. This phenomenon was, in part, due to the expectations of the European Union, which pressured its future members to align their understanding of the Shoah with what Western democracies considered the dominant narrative. A narrative which recognised that the Holocaust was not only a German project, that all European nations were also, to some extent, responsible for the Jewish catastrophe. Equally important was the long-pending desire for prospective EU nations to take stock of their own national pasts, which until recently had been obfuscated, distorted or simply removed from the curriculum by communist authorities. Finally, nationalisms began to grow across Eastern Europe. The Holocaust was, early on, at the centre of Polish memorial policies because it was the only part of Polish history with a universal meaning. Though few people outside of Poland knew anything about Polish history, almost all had heard of Auschwitz. The Holocaust was, therefore, the only part of Polish history that the Polish authorities had no control over. To gain control over the Holocaust narrative has become the main objective of the "history policy" of the Polish state.

In Poland, the pressures of identity politics resulted in the creation of several institutions charged with the development and enforcement of an official, state-approved version of national history. Foremost among them was the Institute of National Remembrance (Instytut Pamięci Narodowej, or IPN), established by parliament in 1998. Initially, the mandate of the institution was to look at twentieth-century crimes committed against the Polish nation and to prosecute people involved with the communist system during the 1944–1989 period. With time, the mandate has been expanded, and now includes the care of enormous archival holdings transferred into the custody of the institute, and educational activities beefed up with a massive research portfolio. The IPN soon went on a shopping spree, hiring hundreds of professional historians; it became the largest producer of historiography in Poland. Nowadays, the IPN, weaponised by the Polish state with a generous budget, and with more than 2500 employees (including 300 with doctoral and professorial titles) has become the major player on the "memorial" field worldwide. It has also become a clear and present threat to the memory of the Holocaust.

The IPN, from the very beginning, had a distinctly right-wing tilt ("defending the good name of the nation") and, not surprisingly, became a refuge for nationalists of various hues. One IPN employee, Wojciech Muszyński, has openly praised the National Radical Camp, or ONR, one of the most militant, rabidly antisemitic organisations of pre-war Poland.

His colleague Mariusz Bechta – who in 2016 was awarded the Golden Cross of Merit "for the promotion of knowledge about Polish history" – has published many books by fascist authors. Both have doctoral titles in history. It raised few eyebrows, then, when in 2016 Jarosław Szarek, the head of the IPN, declared that Germans, not Poles, were responsible for the 1941 mass murder of the Jews in Jedwabne. A brief explanation: Jedwabne was a town in north-east Poland where the local citizens rounded up all their Jewish neighbours, beat them, tortured them and finally herded them into a large barn and burned them alive. The ideological evolution of the IPN reached its logical conclusion with the appointment in 2021 of Tomasz Greniuch (another PhD in history) to the position of director of the IPN's Wrocław office. Greniuch claims not to be a neo-Nazi but has been photographed giving the Nazi salute and belonged to the overtly fascist ONR. He is an open admirer of Léon Degrelle, the Belgian Nazi collaborator about whom Hitler once said, "If I had a son, I would want him to be like Degrelle." After an international outcry, Greniuch was forced to tender his resignation, but the fact that someone with his background could have been appointed in the first place was a disturbing sign of radicalisation of Polish internal politics.

The IPN is just one of the many state institutions deployed by the Polish authorities to confront people, books and ideas considered threats to the myths, legends, half-truths and straight-out lies energetically promoted today by Polish nationalists. Next to it is the Pilecki Institute, founded in 2017, which might be called IPN-lite, a smaller outfit that works hand in hand with the IPN, attacking independent historians and promoting the myth of "innocent Poland". The Pilecki Institute – active not only in Poland but also abroad, with a branch opened in Berlin and another scheduled to open in New York – has significant funds from the state budget and now offers Western academics grants, financially attractive awards and paid lectures; it pays for translation and publication of their books and, for selected scholars, covers the cost of travel.

> *The issues of memory, history and the Holocaust are an area where Polish politicians come together*

In 2020, the state-funded Roman Dmowski Institute for the Legacy of Polish National Thought was opened. For those less familiar with Polish history, a word of explanation: Roman Dmowski was the founder and leader of Endecja, the Polish National-Democratic Party, and a rabid antisemite who made the struggle against Jews a cornerstone of his political ideology. The Dmowski Institute quickly gained notoriety as a clearing house for the disbursement of government funds (known as the "Patriotic Fund") earmarked for extreme nationalists and their militias. Then there is the Polish Ministry of Foreign Affairs, selling the state historical narrative to foreign audiences through a number of specialised branches. There are also various GONGOs (Government-organised Non-Governmental Organisations), generously subsidised by Polish taxpayers with direct links to the Polish authorities. Although their names sound almost burlesque – The Institute to Combat Anti-Polonism Verba Veritatis or The Redoubt of Defence of the Good Name of the Polish Nation – there is nothing amusing about their activities.

After 2015, the Polish "memorial" museums were drafted into the state-sponsored assault on history. Some of them, such as the Jewish Historical Institute in Warsaw and the Museum of the Second World War in Gdańsk, saw the appointment of new directors – loyal soldiers of the nationalist regime – and swiftly aligned their narratives with the expectations of the authorities. Colossal sums have been committed by the Polish government to building new museums, all of which play a role in the memorial warfare against the history of the Holocaust. In 2016, the Markowa Ulma-Family Museum of Poles Who Saved Jews in World War II opened; the Warsaw Ghetto Museum (introduced by Minister of Culture Piotr Gliński as "the museum of Polish–Jewish love") is scheduled to open in 2025, the huge Museum of Polish History will open later this year in Warsaw, and two museums of Cursed Soldiers (more about them in a moment) opened in 2022. Talk about a memorial offensive!

Since parliamentary elections on 15 October 2023, some things have changed in Poland, and some not so much. At the election, a broad coalition of democratic parties defeated the nationalists who had ruled since 2015. The new government, formed in December, started to restore the badly damaged democracy, seizing control of the state-owned media and crown corporations that during the previous eight years had become nothing more than obedient tools in the hands of the ruling party. Restoring the independence of the judiciary has proved to be a much more complex process and the outcome of this struggle is yet to be determined.

But the issues of memory, history and the Holocaust are an area where Polish politicians, regardless of their political stripes, come together. True, some changes were made. The director of the Pilecki Institute has been fired, and the Dmowski Institute has a new chief, who promised to transform the institution from a centre of ultra-right activism into a hub of democratic education. One lives in hope – and wishes him the best of luck. Finally, some of the most toxic GONGOs have seen transfers of state funds either diminished or cut off altogether.

Otherwise, things remain largely unchanged. Early in 2023, before he was elected as prime minister, Donald Tusk promised to shut down the IPN. It was a promise he chose to forget. At the IPN it is, therefore, business as usual. The same director, with his minions – all of them radical right-wing negationists of the Holocaust – remain in place and continue to act as they did before the democratic electoral victory. The IPN's already bloated budget grew during the current fiscal year from 500 million zlotys (US$125 million) to 600 million zlotys (US$150 million). And a fair portion of this budget is earmarked, as it has been for the last eight years, for Holocaust distortion and denial.

Keeping in mind the memory politics of Poland, it is easier to understand why not one comprehensive museum of the Holocaust has been built in a country where the greatest crime in the history of Europe was committed, and where 3 million Polish citizens of Jewish origin were murdered. There are Holocaust museums in the United States, France, Belgium, Australia, Canada and even distant Argentina. In Poland, however, there is none. Although, considering the message a Polish Holocaust museum would likely want to convey, maybe that's for the better?

Lawfare

Polish state institutions, memorial museums, travelling exhibitions, school curricula and GONGOs all repeat the same message of

Polish national innocence during the Holocaust. Those who fail to understand, or who reject the official narrative of the state, may face laws intended to enforce obedience. These legal regulations, meant to defend the "honour of the nation", are styled after legislation harking back to the 1930s. Originally introduced into the Polish criminal code in 1932 as Article 152, the law called for imprisonment of up to three years for those who "publicly deride or mock the Polish nation or Polish state". During the late 1930s, amid growing nationalism and antisemitism, this law was often applied to Polish Jews. After the war, under Communism, the law was changed to better reflect the new political realities. Article 133 of the criminal code stipulated ten years in prison for those who "publicly try to subvert the unity of the Polish People's Republic with an allied state". It was not difficult to guess which allied state the socialist legislators had in mind.

> *"Those who claim that the Polish nation, or the Polish state, bear responsibility should – of course – be in prison"*

In 1997, after the fall of Communism, Polish lawmakers simply brought back the pre-war regulation. The new Article 133 of the criminal code provides for up to three years in prison for people "slandering the good name of the Polish nation". The definition of this good name is, of course, purely arbitrary and it is up to state prosecutors, and their political masters, to decide if and when to file charges. In 2015, Jan T. Gross, one of the best-known scholars of the Holocaust, a professor of history at Princeton University, opined that "during the war, Poles killed more Jews than they killed Germans". Indisputably true, the statement triggered a furious reaction from the Polish authorities and a lengthy, and ultimately futile, investigation conducted under Article 133 of the criminal code.

In January 2018, the Polish parliament voted in the so-called "Polish Holocaust Law" (to be precise, "Changes to the Law Regarding the Institute of National Remembrance"), which, among many other things, threatened those who "blamed Polish society for crimes committed by the Nazi Third Reich" with prison terms of up to three years. The new law, although styled after Article 133, was much more specific, and had a clearly defined "memorial" target. Perceived as a threat to further study of the Holocaust and an assault on the memory of one of the greatest crimes in human history, the passage of the bill raised protests around the world. On 27 June 2018, in the face of international indignation, the Polish government withdrew the criminal provisions of the bill. Mateusz Morawiecki, then the Polish PM, said in the parliament: "Those who claim that the Polish nation, or the Polish state, bear responsibility for the crimes of World War II should – of course – be in prison. But we have to act bearing in mind international realities". Morawiecki assured the parliament that the Polish state still had enough tools at its disposal to inflict pain on offenders – especially through civil litigation. The new bill made it easier for NGOs to take civil action against "slanderers of the good name of the Polish nation", and such lawsuits could henceforth be filed free of court fees. Indeed, this scenario, or plan of action against Polish historians, was soon tested in Polish courts.

On 9 February 2021, I listened as judge Ewa Jończyk of the Warsaw District Court rendered her judgement in the civil lawsuit filed by Filomena Leszczyńska against the historians Barbara Engelking and Jan Grabowski (i.e. me). The plaintiff claimed that the defendants, in a recently published academic book *Night Without End* (two volumes, 3500 footnotes), slandered the memory of her long-deceased uncle, wrongly accusing him of having betrayed hidden Jews to the Germans during the occupation. On the surface, the case looked like a fairly standard lawsuit, filed by a party wishing to defend the good name of her family. In reality, the case was prepared and financed by the Redoubt of Defence of the Good Name of the Polish Nation, a far-right nationalist organisation serving as a proxy for the Polish state. The judgement covered thirty-seven pages, but a few sentences were of particular significance for historians, and especially for historians of the Holocaust:

In light of the above presented ideas and jurisprudence, we can assume that ascribing to Poles the crimes of the Holocaust committed by the Third Reich can be construed as hurtful and striking at the feeling of identity and of national pride ... This forms among the public opinion a drastically untrue image of Poland and ascribes to Poles characteristics which tear away their dignity and undermine a sense of their own value. To blame Poles for the Holocaust, for the killing of Jews during World War II and for seizing their property, touches on the sphere of the national legacy and, consequently, as completely untrue and hurtful, can impact one's feeling of national dignity, destroying the justified – based on facts – conviction that Poland was the victim of war operations initiated and conducted by the Germans ...

Judge Jończyk's verdict sent a chill down the collective spine of the academic community in Poland and abroad. The decision went far beyond anything the plaintiff asked for, and was a brazen attempt to regulate the behaviour of scholars, researchers and educators. In the opening phrase, the judge warned against "ascribing to Poles the crimes of the Holocaust committed by the Third Reich", which was borrowed word for word from Article 55a of the infamous Polish Holocaust Law. But Judge

Jończyk went further. Here, for the first time, the court decided what had actually happened during the Holocaust in Poland. Or, more precisely, the judge decided what had not happened during the Holocaust. And so, according to the court, during World War II, the Poles did not kill the Jews, and they did not rob them of property.

This came as a surprise to historians of the Shoah, who, for years, had conclusively demonstrated the opposite. The largely uncontested consensus (discounting employees of IPN and the Pilecki Institute) is that segments of Polish society took advantage of, or took part in, the German genocidal plan. To declare that these historical findings were, to quote Judge Jończyk once again, "completely untrue" was disingenuous, false and morally reprehensible. In justification of the verdict, the judge also made repeated references to terms such as "national pride" and "national dignity", which – as we learned – deserved legal protection. Neither expression can be legally defined; national pride and national dignity exist in the eye of the beholder. Should the protection of these terms be entrenched in civil jurisprudence, the possibilities of litigation against scholars would become endless.

> *National pride and national dignity exist in the eye of the beholder*

In the end, we won on appeal. The process took nearly three stressful years and involved a considerable financial burden. A wave of state-sponsored hate accompanied the court proceedings, including relentless attacks by Poland's public TV, radio and press. Confronting the might of a hostile state is not something that scholars are either trained or expected to endure. Hearing the news about the decision of the higher court, Zbigniew Ziobro, who was then Polish minister of justice, could not contain himself. He issued a public statement:

> According to the Appellate Court the authors of the book *Night Without End* are academics, so they can lie without punishment. They can transform a hero into a criminal, and a Pole who helped the Jews into someone who was co-responsible for their deaths. It not only brings shame to the court, it is a judicial coup d'état against justice itself.

Przemysław Czarnek, who was Polish minister of science and education, was equally blunt: "*Night Without End* is an anti-Polish rag." Karol Nawrocki, the recently appointed chief of the IPN, declared in an interview that "the authors of *Night Without End* are haters and academic frauds". These comments reflected the moral and ethical bearing of Polish nationalist politicians engaged in Holocaust negationism.

There are laws that do not have to be enforced. It is enough that they are on the books, ready to be used against offending historians, educators, teachers. Nothing more is needed to create a chilling atmosphere, which stifles research into controversial aspects of a nation's past. We will never know how many books will not be written, or how many graduate students will steer clear of "restricted" topics, choosing instead fields of work that are less exposed to the hostile attention of state institutions. If authorities can put through the legal grinder two senior and internationally recognised academics, junior scholars will ask themselves, what might happen to lesser-known defendants? In this way, the Polish state has already won a major battle.

Blaming the victim

In February 2018 then Polish prime minister Mateusz Morawiecki took part in the annual Munich Security Conference. During a panel discussion, Ronen Bergman, a prominent Israeli journalist, and son of Holocaust survivors, confronted the Polish leader about the criminal charges legislated by his parliament against people talking about the role of the Poles in the Holocaust. "Am I going to be criminally charged," Bergman wanted to know, "if I speak about Polish complicity?"

"You're not going to be seen as criminal [if you] say that there were Polish perpetrators, as there were Jewish perpetrators, as there were Russian perpetrators as well as Ukrainian perpetrators – not only German perpetrators," Morawiecki responded. It was not a good answer.

By "Jewish perpetrators", Morawiecki most likely was referring to members of the Judenräte and the Jewish Ghetto Police, the Jüdischer Ordnungsdienst. Placing on equal footing Polish or Ukrainian voluntary perpetrators and Jews in the ghettos is disingenuous at best, and borders on Holocaust denial at worst. The IPN followed the same line of reasoning in a tweet – since removed – implying that the Jewish police were complicit in the detection and death of Emanuel Ringelblum, a Jewish-Polish historian who survived in hiding in Warsaw until March 1944. The IPN conveniently forgot that Ringelblum was detected not by Jewish policemen (who, by March 1944, in Warsaw, were long dead) but by members of a unit of the Polish Criminal Police, who specialised in hunting down hidden Jews.

Tomasz Panfil, chief of the public education department of the IPN office in Lublin, went on record saying that: "Jews did not have it all that bad in the beginning of the German occupation in Poland" and that the "Jewish councils were a form of Jewish self-government". The fact is that Jews were robbed, humiliated, imposed upon and killed from the beginning of the occupation, and Jewish councils, whose members often had to accept the appointment under penalty of death, were simple tools in the hands of the Germans. Both statements are not only proof of shocking ignorance, but also an offence to the memory of the dead. Another form of blaming the victim builds on the alleged Jewish–Bolshevik alliance (known as "Judeocommune") against Polish patriotic elements during the 1939–1941 period, when east Poland was occupied by the Soviet Union.

Other negationists close to, or working for, the IPN claim that one of the reasons Poles were reluctant to offer shelter to Jews was Jewish duplicity and ingratitude. If captured, Jews would betray the trust of their rescuers and reveal their names

> **With the help of Wikipedia, this kind of Holocaust distortion started to make an impact internationally**

to the Germans. There was also the Jewish Gestapo to consider: Jews who worked openly for the German police, whole networks active in the cities and rural areas, tricking Poles into offering help and denouncing them swiftly to the Germans. Most of it is sheer nonsense. One Wikipedia article, "Collaboration in German-Occupied Poland", describes:

a 70-strong group led by a Jewish collaborator called Hening [which] was tasked with operating against the Polish resistance, and was quartered at the Gestapo's Warsaw headquarters on ulica Szucha Street [sic]. Similar groups and individuals operated in towns and cities across German-occupied Poland – including Józef Diamand in Kraków.

The alleged group led by Hening is unknown to historians of Warsaw Jewry, and the group of Jewish collaborators led by Józef Diamant (not Diamand) in Kraków is simple fabrication. Unfortunately, this kind of Holocaust distortion is both frequent and popular in the public and political discourse in Poland and, regrettably, with the help of Wikipedia, it started to make an impact internationally.

Wikipedia and the Holocaust

Several years ago, some students in my Holocaust classes at the University of Ottawa started to ask questions that had little to do with our meetings and even less with the assigned readings. The questions revolved around the issue of Jewish complicity during the Shoah. I soon learned that the root of the problem was Wikipedia – and, more specifically, Wikipedia articles dealing with Jewish–Polish relations during World War II. The deeper I probed, the greater was my concern. The articles on English-language Wikipedia read as if they were produced by the propagandists working for the Polish state apparatus, and repeated historical myths and fallacies espoused by Polish nationalists. Whether one likes it or not, Wikipedia is one of the most heavily used websites in the world, a place where most of us start and finish the quest for information. The distortion, misinformation and plain lies are being consumed by audiences numbering in the millions. Some of these articles were being accessed tens of thousands of times per month. Nothing that historians produce and publish in respected academic reviews comes close to the reach of Wikipedia.

There were four themes in which the site's treatment of history was painfully skewed. First was the false equivalence narrative suggesting that Poles and Jews suffered equally in World War II. Second, Polish antisemitism was presented as a marginal phenomenon, and Wikipedia inflated (sometimes grotesquely) the role of Polish society in saving Jews. Third, antisemitic tropes about Jewish and communist conspiracies against Poland and Poles: the articles were full of them. Finally, the scale of Jewish collaboration with the Nazis was grossly exaggerated, to make it seem an important part of the German policy of the extermination of European Jewry. Since the information on Wikipedia must be sourced and footnoted, the editors involved in falsification and distortion of the historical narrative relied on weak or unreliable sources, misquoted the reliable ones, overquoted marginal authors and ignored mainstream publications.

Working with Shira Klein, a historian from Chapman University who specialises in digital media, I spent two years trying to understand what was being falsified on Wikipedia, and – most importantly – how it was possible in the first place. Wikipedia is, at least in theory, a self-governing organism, whose legions of volunteer editors add their own contributions and make sure that misinformation and errors are weeded out and purged from the narrative through a collective effort. Judging by the content of investigated articles, however, the system had failed badly. It came as a surprise to us that there were three areas flagged by Wikipedia as especially sensitive, for which the right to make changes was restricted to editors with the highest level of "editorial seniority": the Palestinian–Israeli conflict, the Pakistan–India conflict and ... Polish–Jewish relations during World War II. Despite these restrictions, or safeguards, the content of articles dealing with Polish–Jewish relations during the Holocaust was truly appalling.

What happened on Wikipedia, we found out, was that a small group of ideologically driven, experienced editors, working in tandem, was able to dominate the field, effectively blocking and intimidating other editors and preventing them from restoring balance to the narrative. There was no evidence of any official involvement of the Polish state in this sordid affair, although – given the stakes, and the massive impact of Wiki articles on countless thousands of readers – it is only a question of time before that happens. Wikipedia's weakness has already been noticed by the Polish government, as shown in a leaked email exchange between advisers to then Polish prime minister Mateusz Morawiecki concerning the Hebrew-language Wikipedia.

It was in March 2018, when, in the wake of the Holocaust Law, diplomatic relations between Poland and Israel were fraught. Morawiecki's adviser wrote to his chief of staff, referring to Joanna Hofman, who was the director of the Polish Institute in Tel Aviv at the time:

> Ms. Joanna Hofman (our former ambassador in Helsinki) is a very sensible person and she understands the situation. I asked her to find someone who could start to position the Israeli sites in Google and to correct the Hebrew entries in Wikipedia. We need to be super discreet on this score, and she [Hofman] is aware of that … she will need a larger budget to cover this expense. It can be arranged if the Foreign Office allocates more money.

Even in the absence of state-funded distortion, the Wikipedia articles feed their unsuspecting readers information about the alleged Jewish complicity in the Holocaust, about strong links of Jews to Communism and about the benign character of Polish antisemitism, and praise the enormous efforts of ethnic Poles in rescuing their Jewish co-citizens during the Shoah.

The Righteous Defence

Until the Russian invasion of Ukraine, the so-called "dignity file", also known as the "defence of the good name of the nation", was the only issue on which Polish nationalists came together with the representatives of the democratic opposition. This united stand, which builds a bridge between the Polish left and right – extending from communists to fascists, and including the parties of the moderate centre – has a long historical tradition, and the strongest pillar supporting this construct is, undoubtedly, the poorly construed idea of raison d'état, or the "greater good of the state", which is often laced with antisemitism.

Voting patterns in the Polish parliament confirm this pernicious phenomenon. In January 2018, Polish parliamentarians overwhelmingly voted in favour of the Polish Holocaust Law, one of the more disgraceful pieces of legislation in recent memory. In fact, only four members of the Sejm voted against it, while 409 either voted in favour or abstained. The same sentiment of unity allowed Polish parliamentarians to acknowledge and to honour as "true patriots" the extreme nationalists and murderers of Jews from the Holy Cross Brigade of the National Armed Forces and to recognise as heroes the "cursed soldiers" (post-1945 anticommunist fighters, many of whom are well-documented killers of Jews).

This united front of Holocaust negationism started practically as soon as the war was over. On 4 July 1946, in Kielce, an angry mob driven to frenzy by false rumours of a blood libel – in this case, news that Jews had murdered a Polish boy for ritual purposes – initiated a pogrom. In a horrible display of senseless violence, the crowd stormed a temporary shelter for the few local survivors of the Holocaust. Before the day was over, forty-nine Jews had died at the hands of their Polish neighbours, soldiers and militiamen. The wave of shocking violence spilled over to other Polish cities, claiming further victims. In the aftermath of the Kielce massacre, any remaining Polish Jews fled Poland in terror and panic. For all practical purposes, Poland had become *Judenrein*, cleansed of the Jews. In Kielce, the Final Solution to the Jewish Question, promised earlier by Adolf Hitler,

> **For all practical purposes, Poland had become Judenrein, *cleansed of the Jews***

had been brought to its conclusion by local citizens, fourteen months after the fall of the Third Reich.

A post-mortem followed. The communists blamed the reactionary forces, while the nationalists (and popular opinion) perceived the pogrom as a communist provocation, a conspiracy to tarnish the image of Poland abroad to weaken Western support for the democratic forces in communist-dominated Poland. Even the independent Catholic press saw the pogrom as a complete aberration, an inexcusable exception from the otherwise welcoming attitudes demonstrated by Polish society to Jews during the war. That the pogrom in Kielce could have been an expression of virulent, popular antisemitism – which had been strong before the war and had matured into a deadly ideology of murder under German influence – was something no one could acknowledge. Asking serious questions about the moral condition of Polish society was a losing proposition. No one, from left to right, was prepared to admit that a blood libel, the age-old legend of Jews draining blood from Christian children, could trigger the deadliest pogrom in post-war European history. To make matters worse, all of this happened at the epicentre of the Holocaust, in an unfortunate geographic location where everyone had stared the unprecedented genocide straight in the face, and claiming ignorance was not an option.

In the aftermath of the Kielce pogrom, Catholic intelligentsia attempted to downplay the scale and importance of Polish antisemitism, while the communist authorities began to spin their own web of lies. As soon as the war was over, it was time to count the dead. By early 1946 the results were in: according to official counts, about 3 million Polish Jews and 1.8 million ethnic Poles had died at the hands of the Germans. By any measure, these were staggering numbers, but the large difference between the Polish and Jewish losses worried the communist authorities. After 1944, the communists were broadly perceived as agents of the Soviets and as "Jewish lackeys". Publishing that Polish losses were so much lower than the Jewish ones could – the authorities feared –

Berman requested that Jewish and Polish losses be declared equal: 3 million dead each

trigger a backlash against the government. In early 1946, Jakub Berman, chief of the feared Polish communist security apparatus, issued an order to establish Polish and Jewish losses as on par. "Should we recognise the fact that three million Jews were murdered," said Berman, "then we would need to sharply increase the numbers of Polish dead." In a policy memo titled "Establish the Number of Dead at Six Million", Berman requested that Jewish and Polish losses be declared equal: 3 million dead each. It had nothing to do with historical accuracy, but was the earliest demonstration of the phenomenon known today as Holocaust envy. The estimates of Polish losses, pulled out of a hat by Berman in 1946, quickly became official. And today, seventy-eight years later, they continue to be part of the distorted, although widely accepted, vision of the past.

In March 1968, two decades after the Kielce pogrom, the ruling communists initiated a vicious antisemitic campaign. The campaign was a corollary to the 1967 Six-Day War, won by Israel, which brought about a furious reaction from the Soviet Union and from many states of the "socialist camp", including Poland. Wiesław Gomułka, first secretary of the Polish United Workers' Party, in a notorious televised speech, said:

> In view of the fact that Israel's aggression against Arab countries has been met with applause in Zionist circles of Jewish-Polish citizens, I would like to state the following: we did not make obstacles for Polish citizens of Jewish nationality to move to Israel if they wished to do so. We stand on the position that every Polish citizen should have only one homeland – the People's Poland.

Although primarily meant to settle scores between various factions within the Polish United Workers' Party, the campaign spilled into other organisations and escalated into massive purges, which became front-page news. Thousands of people lost their jobs and close to 20,000 were forced to leave Poland, and most of their possessions, with one-way "stateless persons" travel documents. Interestingly, the antisemitic campaign of 1968 was the only major communist-driven propaganda initiative that resonated with the broad masses of Polish society.

This time, however, the victims were people whose link to Jewishness was tenuous at best. After all, the vast majority of those who had preserved their Jewish identity had left Poland, either after the Kielce pogrom or after 1955, during the so-called political thaw following Stalin's death. The victims of the March 1968 campaign had, for the most part, made a conscious decision to leave their Jewishness behind, to blend in with mainstream society and to espouse the national ethos (sometimes even to convert to Catholicism), in order to become "real" Poles. Now, they learned that it was up to the authorities to determine their identity, and their Polishness was found wanting. Shortly before the war, Hitler's deputy Hermann Göring had announced: "*Wer Jude ist, bestimme ich!*" (It is for me to decide who is a Jew!) In March 1968, Polish communists decided that Göring had been on to something.

The antisemitic campaign raised concern in Europe and beyond. Among the thousands of stateless refugees knocking on the doors of Western embassies in search of visas and safe haven were well-known intellectuals, writers and artists. Press and politicians expressed indignation, and international organisations issued harsh condemnation of the discriminatory and racist policies of the Polish state. The ugly face of Polish antisemitism was again the talk of the town. In Poland, the reaction was swift. Voices were raised in defence of the good name of the nation, smeared by the "capitalist and anti-Polish" press. "Jews are ungrateful", "Poles saved the Jews", "the Polish nation suffered as much as the Jews under the occupation", "millions of Poles came to the rescue of the Jews!" The communist-controlled press and state broadcasters were unequivocal. The Catholic press, and the Catholic Church, expressed similar sentiments. An idea gained traction: that the numbers (invented, if required) of Poles allegedly rescuing Jews would restore the good name of the nation. That's when the exotic notion of millions of Polish Righteous became an inalienable part of the distortionist message. I like to call this particular kind of history negation "The Righteous Defence".

The Righteous Defence is not only based on the premise of Polish virtue; it also implies Jewish ingratitude. In 1968, the Polish newspapers were filled with articles like one entitled "This Is What We Get in Return! Poles Helping the Jews", published by the daily newspaper *Zielony Sztandar*:

It is with disgust and astonishment that I read about the slanders and smear campaigns orchestrated by various foreign Jewish circles, accusing us Poles of helping the Nazis to murder the Jews. It is difficult to imagine something more disgusting, and more untrue about our society. We, former soldiers of the Resistance, are appalled at the slanders raised against us in Israel and elsewhere. So this is the payback for all the help given to the Jews? For all the sacrifice? Where are those whose lives we have saved? Why these Jews, who today live in Israel, the USA, in Germany and elsewhere, why do they remain silent?

The chorus of praise for Poles rescuing the Jews was led by communo-fascists such as Mieczysław Moczar and Ryszard Gontarz, people known for their aggressive antisemitism.

Even emigré circles, made up of staunch anti-communists, chose to defend the good name of the nation, a task which – at least for a while – trumped their struggle against Communism. It is hard to imagine foes more bitter than hard-line communists in Warsaw and expatriate Polish politicians and soldiers living in exile in the West. Nevertheless, in 1968, their voices joined the same improbable chorus of Righteous Defence. Both sides were ready to sacrifice historical truth and common decency at the altar of the variously construed Polish raison d'état, and in defence of the myth of the universality of Polish rescue attempts during the Holocaust. Kazimierz Iranek-Osmecki was one of the heroes of the patriotic Polish resistance living in exile, in Great Britain. In 1968, he published a book, *He Who Saves One Life*, moved by the fact that:

> such a study is doubly important now since the press, both in the West and in Israel, has made many accusations about the attitude of the Polish nation. The press contends that the Poles were passive, that they looked with indifference on the extermination of the Jews, and that they even collaborated with the Germans in the crime.

Similar studies, articles, books and documentary films, produced by both Catholics and communists, started to proliferate in Poland.

The feel-good narrative based on Righteous Defence hit a bump in 2000, after the publication of Jan T. Gross's book *Neighbors*. This thin volume, drawing heavily on the testimony of Jewish survivors, told the story of Jedwabne, the town in northeast Poland where, in July 1941, the local Poles, not without German encouragement, decided to kill their Jewish neighbours. It was not a pogrom, defined as a recurring orgy of violence visited by gentiles upon Jewish communities for centuries. The goal of the Polish citizens of Jedwabne was to kill them all, to eradicate the Jews from their city. In the course of one day, the Poles rounded up as many of their Jewish neighbours as they could (estimates vary from several hundred to more than 1000 people), killed some of them in the streets, and closed the rest in a large barn, poured in gasoline and burned them alive.

Gross's book sent shockwaves through the nation. How could "a nation without a Quisling" – as many referred to Poland, and its absence of political collaboration – take part in, or execute, such a heinous crime? It was a time of soul-searching, of heated debates on TV and the radio. Copies of *Neighbors* could be purchased in supermarkets, in the express-checkout lanes. The IPN, whose stated mission

> **Massive resources of the state have been committed to reinforcing the myth of Poles rescuing Jews**

was to investigate "crimes committed against the Polish nation" had no choice but to start looking into the crimes committed *by* the Polish nation. But the period of critical reflection ended as abruptly as it had begun.

The negationist reaction to Gross's book was based on several key premises. For one, said the proponents of innocent Poland, it must have been the Germans who were responsible. In Jedwabne, if there were some Poles involved, they surely acted under German orders and were, most likely, a few bad apples, criminals, who can be found in every society. The great majority of the Polish townspeople had nothing to do with the event, it was argued. Second, there is no way that so many Jews could have been forced into that barn. Gross lies about the number of victims, so he lies about everything else too, said the defenders of the good name of the nation. "Jews had it coming," argued those who wanted to bring back the spectre of Judeocommune. Third, Jedwabne was an aberration, they said, an outrageous exception to the otherwise dominant pattern of good relations between Poles and Jews. The news that Jedwabne was just one of more than twenty locations in the Polish eastern borderlands where, in the summer of 1941, Poles murdered their Jewish neighbours, did little to change this line of reasoning.

Finally, there was the Righteous Defence. Massive resources of the state have been committed to reinforcing the myth of Poles rescuing Jews, both for internal consumption and for international use. The results, unfortunately – from a historian's point of view – were encouraging for the state. The polls confirmed it again and again. Over the years, Poles have been asked a question: "Who suffered more during the last war, the Jewish or the Polish nation?" In 1992, 46 per cent of those polled replied that Jews suffered more. By 2021, this opinion was shared only by

28 per cent of respondents. The percentage of those who thought that both nations suffered equally grew steadily: from 32 per cent in 1992 to 51 per cent in 2021. Finally, in 2021, a stunning 71 per cent of Polish respondents came to the conclusion that, during World War II, Poles suffered as much as, or more than, the Jews.

Professor Marek Kucia, a sociologist at Jagiellonian University in Cracow, has been researching these issues for decades. In 2021, he found that the overwhelming majority (84 per cent) of Poles were convinced that their ancestors, under the occupation, helped the Jews "as much as they could". The fact that 99 per cent of Polish Jews perished in the Shoah does not seem to bother people anymore. Despite the occasional road bump, such as the publication of *Neighbors*, defence of the good name of the nation seems to have won the day, trumping historical evidence and the existing scholarship, making Poland a leader in Holocaust denial and distortion worldwide.

The triumphant march of negationism comes with a hefty price tag, which should have us all concerned. According to Kucia's studies, 55 per cent of Poles think that "Jews have too much influence in the world", and 41 per cent declared that Jews cannot change their bad national characteristics, "because that's their nature". Nineteen per cent claimed, at the same time, that "war was a horrible thing, but it is good that as a result we do not have as many Jews in Poland as we used to have". This was the opinion shared by every fifth person polled in 2021, in a country which, three generations earlier, was the killing ground for 5 out of the 6 million victims of the Holocaust.

Indifference was impossible

Michał Okoński, who complained about my "lamentable" research, referred to my estimates of the number of Jews either killed by their Polish co-citizens or denounced by them to the Germans. On the basis of nearly two decades of research, I established this number at around 200,000 people, which, I argue, is a conservative estimate. Nevertheless, this estimate galvanises Polish public opinion like few other historical issues, and forms a narrow bridge upon which people of all political colours, such as the Catholic journalist Okoński and the fascist politician Braun, come together in defence of the good name of their nation. To grasp the essence of the problem, a few words about history are in order.

Historians of the Final Solution in Poland divide the Holocaust into three, often overlapping, periods: the early occupation and ghettoisation, the liquidations of the ghettos, and the Judenjagd, or the hunt for the Jewish survivors. The periodisation differs according to whether one looks at the eastern territories, the areas annexed into the Reich, or the central parts of Poland, where the Germans established a buffer state known as the

Generalgouvernement. Without going into detail, however, the first period ended in 1942, the second lasted from 1942 to early 1943, and the third started whenever the local ghettos were liquidated, usually in mid- to late 1942, and lasted until the end of the war.

Poland was ground zero of the Holocaust: it is where Jews slated for death were brought from across occupied Europe. More importantly, the Germans were not simply "delivering" Jews to the extermination camps. First, they had to force millions of starving men, women and children out of their homes, then herd them into the cattle cars and, finally, drag them into the gas chambers. Each step of the way, the Jews were likely to resist. Unlike the Jews

Sometimes separated by nothing more than barbed wire, the Poles had a first-hand view of the genocide

of Western Europe, Polish Jews were aware early on of the real meaning of the term "deportations to the east". In order to terrorise the Jewish masses, to cow them into submission and break their will to resist, the liquidation actions (known in German as *Aktionen*) were conducted with unprecedented brutality. The streets of Polish cities quite literally ran with blood and, during the horrible hours and days of the *Aktionen*, between 10 and 20 per cent of the Jews living in the ghetto were murdered there, or on the way to the nearest railway station. In some areas, especially those more distant from the railway tracks, such as parts of the Lublin district, the Germans are known to have murdered up to one half of all "deported" Jews in situ.

During the *Aktionen*, around 10 per cent of Jews, or close to 250,000 people, fled the ghettos and went into hiding on the "Aryan side". Fewer than 30,000 survived until liberation. The fate of the remaining 220,000 was, in the great majority of cases, settled by the decisions of Polish gentiles. In addition to the Jews who perished during the period of Judenjagd, we need to consider the Jews who died during the liquidation actions, during the second phase of the Holocaust, inside the ghettos, with the involvement of Poles. There were Polish volunteer firefighters who joined the Germans during and after liquidation of the ghettoes, and there were Polish collaborationist "blue" policemen who went hunting for Jewish survivors once the German forces left the liquidated ghettos. And there were crowds of "bystanders", uncounted thousands of them, who entered the ghettos looking for loot – and for hidden Jews, who could fetch a good price. All these victims need to be taken into account, and this makes my estimate of 200,000 Jews who perished with the involvement of the Poles a conservative one.

There were very few sealed ghettos in Poland, such as the ones in Warsaw, Kraków or Łódź. Hundreds of other ghettos were open, with the gentile population living virtually next door to their Jewish neighbours. Sometimes separated by nothing more than barbed wire or a flimsy fence, the Poles had a first-hand view of the genocide. Once the liquidations began, some closed the curtains and pretended not to see, others took advantage of the Jewish catastrophe and robbed whatever movables they could lay their hands on. Some Poles joined the Germans and started to hunt down Jews holed up in ingenious hideouts, inside the ghettos. Still others eyed with interest the houses and apartments which had now become available. And very few, very courageous people tried to offer meaningful help to the dying.

Remaining indifferent in these circumstances was simply impossible. Elżbieta Janicka, a scholar from the Polish Academy of Sciences, summed it up:

> Contrary to prevailing assumptions, the main problem with the dominant Polish attitude towards Jews was not a lack of help. Nor was it passivity or indifference. It was the fact that it was a common occurrence for Poles to identify Jews, expel them from subsequent hideouts, rob them, denounce them, often hand them over to the Germans, and in many cases murder them. Paradoxically, if the Poles had been mostly indifferent and passive, the majority – not a tiny minority – of Jews seeking refuge from the Germans on the so-called Aryan side would have survived.

A few years ago, I was sorting through the papers of my late father, a Holocaust survivor. I came across his letter dated 2 September 1973, addressed to Kazimierz Koźniewski, a heroic underground soldier during the war, and an influential writer during the People's Republic. Reading the yellowed note, a copy punched through the carbon paper of a typewriter, I had a sense of déjà vu. The letter was about pre-war antisemitism, about how, during the war, Polish society was united against the Germans – with one exception: there was no widespread condemnation of the German treatment of Jews. My father wrote about the theft of Jewish property, about the constant fear of blackmail and the impunity of blackmailers. In the Polish language a special word – *shmaltsovnik* – had to be coined during the occupation to describe a new profession: that of people who preyed on the Jews in hiding.

He wrote:

[F]or those who took this risk [saving Jews] nobly, it was a difficult and risky necessity to act, on their own, each separately. They always had to hide their Christian compassion and conspire much more carefully with their fellow Poles than those who, for example, hid wounded partisans. On the matter of hiding a partisan, society was in solidarity – but not on the matter of hiding a Jew! Surely you have not forgotten such common, horrifying sentences at the time: "Nevertheless, we should put up a golden monument to Hitler – he's doing our dirty work for us!" And then, when the ghetto joined the final battle and burned in a roar of gunfire, when Warsaw was strewn with charred scraps of paper, and good people clenched their fists in painful helplessness – what was the typical reaction of the Warsaw crowd? "Ha-ha! The Jew-boys are fighting? O, really!?" Many of those who surreptitiously knocked (or perhaps you don't know how we felt being tracked down as animals) were met with doors slammed shut in horror; often with mockery, we had insults thrown in our faces; dogs were set upon us, and sometimes we saw the characteristic – familiar to each of us – sinister glint in the eye, which meant: "run away – this man will give you away!" Hyenas are not extinct, they have not fled – they live peacefully among us as typical and respected members of society, not unlike their much more blood-stained counterparts in West and East Germany.

The arguments raised by my father more than half a century ago were forcefully rejected then, and they are still rejected today. Eighty years of rejection and denial.

Anti-communism trumps antisemitism

Samek Abrahamer was a survivor. He survived the Holocaust in Warsaw, in hiding, together with his wife and daughter, on the Aryan side of the city. In early 1944, running out of money and fearing denunciation and death, the family escaped to Hungary. Their flight from Warsaw, through much of Poland, over the Slovak mountains and into Budapest, must have been a harrowing experience, but they made it to the Hungarian capital. In the winter of 1944, Hungary was widely perceived as a refuge, a safe haven for Jews, especially when compared to the killing fields of Poland. In March 1944, however, the Wehrmacht entered Hungary and soon the massive deportations of Hungarian Jews began. All in all, between May and July 1944, more than 430,000 Jews were sent from Hungary to Auschwitz-Birkenau. Very few survived. The Abrahamers again managed to avoid the hunt, and soon after liberation, in winter 1945, they returned to Poland, to their native Kraków. Samek came back to reclaim the businesses of his father, Israel Abrahamer, a wealthy Kraków miller, industrialist and philanthropist who had been murdered by the Germans in August 1942.

Full disclosure: Samek's brother Jozue Abrahamer was my grandfather. In 1945, unwilling to go back to his real name, Jozue decided to legalise his "Aryan" papers, which had served him so well during the war, and officially changed his name to Czesław Grabowski. Samek, on the other hand, decided to keep his Jewish name. These decisions, in either case, could not have been easy. After the war, and despite liberation, Poland remained a scary place for Jews. Historians have no precise numbers, but during the 1945–47 period anywhere between 1500 and 2000 Jews were murdered. Members of various anti-communist organisations targeted them, later explaining away the murders with "patriotic" excuses of fighting Communism or the Judeocommune. Scores died in the "railway action" (*akcja pociągowa*), in which posses of bandits roamed trains looking for Jews. The victims were killed by being thrown off the trains, or were marched off and executed close to the tracks. And then there were the pogroms. First, in June 1945, Rzeszów, then in August 1945, Kraków, and finally, the bloodiest, in Kielce, in July 1946. This was the social and political climate in which Samek Abrahamer took over the businesses of his murdered father. But not for long.

> *These murderers are treated as heroes, whose moral choices should set an example for the young generation*

On 8 April 1946, shortly before 6 p.m., Samek left the mill in Zielonki (a suburb of Kraków) in the company of his secretary, the twenty-year-old Zofia Scheinborn. They took a droshky, a horse-drawn cart which then substituted for a taxi. Outside the gate of the mill compound, on the Kraków highway, three men waited in ambush. They stopped the droshky, ordered the cart driver to stand aside, and opened fire on the passengers. Samek was shot in the head and the chest; Zofia was repeatedly shot in the chest and the abdomen. Both died of their wounds the next day, in hospital. According to the report filed later by the militia, the murderers spared the life of the Polish droshky driver and stole whatever they could find on the victims: 4000 zlotys, watches, Samek's wedding ring, two pairs of gloves, a woman's purse, a leather briefcase and two winter coats. Samek was buried in a ruined and plundered Jewish cemetery on Miodowa Street. His brother Jozue (now Czesław) did not attend the funeral: he was too afraid to board a train from Warsaw – where he lived – to Kraków.

A few months later the murderers – involved in the killings of several other Jews – were caught by the militia. As the investigators soon learned, all belonged to the Battalion of Anti-Comintern Self-defence (*Batalion Samoobrony Antykominternowskiej*), one of the many units of the anti-communist and "patriotic" resistance. Neither Samek nor his secretary were communists. But they were wealthy Jews, which, in the eyes of Polish anti-communist fighters, was more than enough reason to kill them.

In today's Poland, these murderers are treated as heroes, whose moral choices should set an example for the young generation.

Called Cursed Soldiers (*żołnierze wyklęci*), they symbolise the struggle of Polish society against Soviet-imposed Communism. Józef Kuraś, who went by the noms de guerre Eagle and Fire, was perhaps the most iconic and celebrated among the Cursed Soldiers; he fought the Germans and, later, the communists. For Kuraś, the struggle against communists involved killing Jews: he made no distinction between them. In May 1946, in one of the more notorious cases, his men killed a group of Jews fleeing Poland. Eleven people were executed, while seven others, though wounded, managed to flee. Women, men, children, survivors of the Holocaust. It so happens that the killers of Samek Abrahamer and Zofia Scheinborn belonged to Kuraś's underground resistance network.

> *Kuraś's deeds are celebrated in museums, and Polish scouts take part in raids and expeditions bearing his name*

Józef Kuraś is nowadays hailed as a national hero. In 2006 then president Lech Kaczyński unveiled a monument to him in Zakopane, in southern Poland. In 2011, long before the authoritarian turn in Polish policies, Kaczyński's successor, President Bronisław Komorowski, declared 1 March the National Day of Remembrance of the Cursed Soldiers. Kuraś's deeds are celebrated in museums, and Polish scouts take part in raids and expeditions bearing his name. In March 2023, the Polish mint issued a new ten-zloty coin, in sterling silver, with his portrait. Beneath it a legend reads: "They acted as one should have" (*Zachowali się jak trzeba*). In Poland, killing Jews is no longer odious. Killing Jews is irrelevant, as long as the murderers can present impeccable anti-communist credentials.

Morawiecki, then the prime minister, drove the point home during the 2018 Munich Security Conference, when he chose to lay a wreath on the grave of soldiers of the Holy Cross Brigade. This was the only major unit of the Polish resistance which, in the winter of 1944–45, withdrew to the west, together with the retreating Nazi forces. In 1944 the Holy Cross Brigade struck a deal with the Germans and focused on fighting the communist resistance and killing Jews. Taking advantage of his stay in Munich, the Polish PM could have visited the Dachau concentration camp, or the monument commemorating the young people of the "White Rose" anti-Nazi group. Instead, he chose to lay flowers on the graves of people for whom the struggle against Jews and communists was more important than the struggle against the Nazis. Shortly before his visit, closing the circle, the Polish Parliament had voted unanimously to recognise the soldiers of the Holy Cross Brigade as "true patriots who had served their Fatherland well".

Polonising Treblinka, part I: then

Treblinka death camp is the second-largest Jewish cemetery in the world, after Auschwitz. Here, on a small patch of land, hidden in the forests of eastern Poland, the Germans murdered close to 900,000 Jews. The victims were brought to this remote area known as Podlasie from around Poland and other occupied countries by train, sometimes up to 10,000 people per transport. Usually, the trains waited for hours, sometimes days, at the Treblinka railway station, before the wagons, with their human cargo, were pushed into the camp nearby. The conditions in the wagons were beyond description, with 150 people packed in each, dying of wounds, heat and thirst. Between July 1942 and August 1943, the small railway station became a true gateway to hell. Out of the 900,000 Jews brought there, little more than 100 survived the war. Some decided to share their stories.

On 23 August 1942, during the liquidation of the Warsaw Ghetto, Jankiel Wiernik was caught in a manhunt and, the next day, found himself in Treblinka. His testimony, among the earliest to be published, appeared during the war, in 1944, after his successful escape:

> The train moved in the morning, and we rolled into the Treblinka railway station. It was a hot day. We could hardly

breathe. We were horribly thirsty. I looked out the window. The peasants brought water and asked for 100 zlotys per bottle. I had no money, other than a few silver coins with [former leader of Poland] the marshal's face, which I kept for sentimental reasons. So I had to forgo water. Others, however, paid the money.

Eddie Weinstein, from the town of Łosice, arrived at Treblinka Station on 25 August 1942, a day after Wiernik. He described the situation on the ramp:

We were horribly thirsty and we had no idea what would happen with us. But even in these circumstances money, and jewellery even more so, were still appreciated. The Poles who worked on the station came to an SS soldier and asked him for permission to bring water to the thirsty people. The soldier gave his consent. So they brought buckets of water close to the wagons and started filling empty bottles handed over by the passengers. For this, they wanted good payment. They clearly considered Polish bills worthless and they only took hard currency and precious objects, such as rings and brooches. Without them it was impossible to get water. These "merciful" Poles split the profits with the soldiers. Someone in our wagon gave them a few gold coins and in return we received a real treasure: a small bucket of water.

Abram Jakub Krzepicki found himself at the railway station in Treblinka on 26 August 1942, a day after Eddie Weinstein. Eventually, he managed to flee Treblinka, and returned to the Warsaw Ghetto to leave a record:

> The situation in the wagon deteriorated quickly. Water! We begged the railway workers through the window. We offered them a lot of money. It was awful. But we had not enough money to cover the cost of water. People paid 500 and 1000 zlotys for a few sips of water. The railway workers and the auxiliaries took the money. He who had not lived through it, won't believe … I paid 500 zlotys – more than one half of what I had – and received a jar (half a litre) of water. When I started drinking, a woman rushed to me, crying that her child had fainted. I drank and I could not take the jar away from my mouth. The woman bit me on the hand as hard as she could. She wanted to force me to stop drinking, to leave some water for her.

There are other Jewish testimonies from the railway station in Treblinka but all agree that for the local railway workers who could gain access to death trains, this was a real El Dorado, a mythical city of gold in this remote corner of Podlasie. Murderous greed spilled all over the area. Samuel Rajzman, who had fled Treblinka after the uprising of the Jews in 1943, which broke up the death camp, wrote:

> The peasants around Treblinka were particularly hostile to Jews. They caught the children and led them to Treblinka camp on a rope, like calves, to be murdered. Their reward was 250 grams of sugar, sometimes nothing at all. The villages surrounding Treblinka are today full of treasures in gold taken away from the Jews.

Richard Glazar, another Jewish refugee from Treblinka, noted in his memoirs: "the whole area, in all directions, takes advantage of this enormous slaughterhouse which leaks money. Everybody seems interested in keeping Treblinka going, so it leaves behind its precious byproduct: cash, gold and diamonds." This was Treblinka in 1942 and 1943.

Polonising Treblinka, part II: now

Magdalena Gawin, then Poland's deputy minister of culture and national heritage, arrived at the station in Treblinka on 25 November 2021, eighty years after Wiernik, Rajzman, Krzepicki, Weinstein and 900,000 other Jews. Flanked by officials, members of the press, employees of the Pilecki Institute, which was responsible for the event, four Catholic priests and Rabbi Yehoshua Ellis, who ensured a token but indispensable Jewish presence, she shared an optimistic message of hope. The Jews did not die alone, she said. "This place", she declared, "is so special and so deeply marked by the suffering of thousands of innocent people, that all of us, we should work together so that good can emerge from this tragedy, out of the sacrifice of this young man."

The young man was Jan Maletka, a Polish railway worker from the local village who – according to the employees of the Pilecki Institute – had been shot by the Germans at Treblinka Station for delivering water to the dying Jews. The crucial part, insisted the Pilecki people, was that Maletka acted out of the goodness of his heart. While there is no question that Maletka was shot at the station on 20 August 1942, there is not a shred of credible historical evidence that the young railway worker was trying to help the Jews for altruistic reasons. There is, however, overwhelming evidence from Jewish survivors that water at the railway platform in Treblinka was not given, but sold to dying Jews at outrageous prices.

To celebrate Polish suffering and sacrifice, Gawin unveiled a monument with a sign in Polish and English which read:

"In memory of Jan Maletka murdered by the Germans on 20 August 1942 for helping Jews. In memory of Jews murdered at the Nazi German Extermination Camp in Treblinka." The monument to the railway worker Jan Maletka and 900,000 anonymous Jews now sits on the former Treblinka railway station, and will remain there until the end of days. In this way, among the religious and secular celebrations, in the company of Catholic priests and a rabbi, one of the last places devoted solely to the memory of Jewish suffering and tragedy was appropriated by Polish officials for the purposes of Polish martyrdom.

The unveiling of the Maletka monument in Treblinka was the most brazen and outrageous – given the location – act of the Pilecki Institute, but it was not its first. The Pilecki Institute has unveiled ten such monuments in the immediate vicinity of the camp, surrounding Treblinka with a "sanitary cordon" of Polish virtue and sacrifice, alleged or real. All these monuments celebrate Poles who sacrificed their lives to rescue Jews. Some of these deeds have been documented by historians, others by the employees of the Pilecki Institute. All are examples of the memorial struggle that takes no prisoners. A struggle in which the spoils go to the living, and where even the dead are offered no quarter.

A similar sanitary cordon of Polish virtue surrounds the impressive building of the POLIN Museum of the History of Polish Jews, in Warsaw. Considered by the authorities as a potential threat to the official historical narrative (without any reason, I would argue), the museum is now held in check by markers I call "memory patches". Along the south side of the museum runs the Irena Sendler Path, named after a courageous Polish woman who helped to save several hundred Jewish children from the Warsaw Ghetto. Next to it is a Jan Karski bench, with a seated figure cast in bronze of the Polish underground courier who carried news about the Holocaust to the indifferent West. There is also a monument to Żegota, the underground organisation to help Jews, and a tree of Polish–Jewish solidarity. Plans are being made to erect – along the northern wall of the museum – a monument devoted to Polish rescuers. Nearby, there is a Park of the Righteous, and, down the road from the museum, the Warsaw municipal authorities transformed a simple intersection into the Roundabout of the Righteous Among the Nations, celebrating gentiles who helped Jews. The roundabout is so compact that the cars can hardly follow the curve of the street, and city buses regularly ignore it, continuing over the elevated central circle. It is not the functionality that counts, however, but the defence of the good name of the nation.

> *It is not the functionality that counts, but the defence of the good name of the nation*

The monuments erected by Pilecki propagandists alone are not enough to appropriate Treblinka for the purpose of Polish national mythology. The memorial takeover is anchored in Treblinka I. Few people know that there were two camps in Treblinka. The first, opened in autumn of 1941, was a labour camp, Treblinka I, which used Jewish and Polish inmates to work in a gravel pit. It was a camp with a brutal regime and, according to less than precise statistics, out of 20,000 people who went through Treblinka I, at least 10,000 died, the vast majority of them Jews. The labour camp was closed in mid-1944, shortly before the arrival of the Red Army. In the spring of 1942, 2 kilometres away, the Germans started construction of Treblinka II, the notorious death camp. The first transport of Jews from the Warsaw Ghetto to be gassed here was on 23 July 1942.

The Polish inmates sent to Treblinka I were usually local peasants arrested by the Germans for failing to deliver quotas of meat, rye or wheat, or accused of black-market operations or other breaches of war-time regulations. The Poles typically were sentenced to fixed terms of hard labour and released once their term was up. The working conditions were appalling, the overseers cruel. While many (around 300, according to rather precise counts) Polish inmates died in Treblinka I, their situation was incomparably better than that of the thousands of Jewish slaves who were sent there, without exception, to die. A local historian left the following description of the largest mass execution in Treblinka I, shortly before the closing of the camp, in the summer of 1944:

> They closed the Polish inmates in the barracks, and the SS and the guards surrounded the area where Jews were being held. Jews were ordered to leave the barracks and lie on the ground, facedown. At that point, there were 550 people in the Jewish part of the camp, including women and children. The Germans selected seventeen highly useful specialists. The guards took the other Jewish prisoners in small groups to the forest, and they executed them.

Today, the execution site is a field of crosses – 296 of them at last count – commemorating the Polish victims of the camp. The great majority of the victims of Treblinka I were Jews, including hundreds of children and teenagers caught outside the Warsaw Ghetto without armbands in the spring of 1942. Not that this message can be conveyed anymore.

On the desk in front of me, there's a book titled *The History of Sad Places, or the Hard Labour Camp Treblinka I*, published in 2022, and intended for Polish schoolchildren who visit the camp. In the entire text the word "Jew" does not appear even once. The inmates, the victims, are all ethnic Poles: "among the prisoners, there were mainly railway workers, carpenters, doctors, tailors, bricklayers". All Poles, as we can gather from their names. I must correct myself: the word "Jew" appears once, in the glossary. The glossary teaches the children that the Jews are "a group of people who now have their own country called Israel. They have the Hebrew language, which they use, and a religion called Judaism." Contrast this with the entry for the Roma and Sinti people, who are "a nation which does not have its own country but has its own customs and language. During the war, German Nazis took away their rights and deported them to death camps, for instance to Treblinka II," The Jews, unlike the Sinti and Roma, are not a nation, and the fact that they have some kind of connection to the place called Treblinka has been judged by the authors altogether irrelevant.

Polish children will learn from *The History of Sad Places* that Treblinka I is a place of Polish suffering, and all its prisoners and victims were Poles. They will not read about the thousands of Jews who perished inside the camp. The person responsible for vetting the content of this intriguing publication is Edward Kopówka, the director of the state museum in Treblinka. The book was financed by the German foundation Der Trägerkreis Schoah-Gedenkstätten from Bielefeld, which supports the erection of Shoah-related monuments in Poland. One can only hope that the German philanthropists did not know their funds helped to shore up the narrative of Holocaust negationism.

This is how Treblinka I, largely Polonised, has become the counterweight to the "Jewish" Treblinka II. Covered with rows of crosses and appropriated for Catholic rituals, the labour camp and the adjacent area are often referred to in Poland as "our Treblinka". One objective of Holocaust distortion is to elevate your own suffering to the level of Jewish suffering. Blending the narratives of Treblinka I and Treblinka II, domesticating the name for your own purposes, are important steps in this direction. Not surprisingly, the full name of the onsite museum is now Treblinka Museum, the Nazi German Extermination and Forced Labour Camp (1941–1944), and the medals it awards give the two Treblinkas equal weight. The Treblinka extermination camp, surrounded by monuments of Polish virtue erected by Pilecki people, has become a place where Holocaust de-judaisation and Holocaust envy come together in the triumphant march of Holocaust distortion.

> *The memorial techniques are as unsophisticated as they are successful*

Polonising Auschwitz

A similar process of Polonisation is underway in Auschwitz. According to polls, close to 50 per cent of Poles primarily associate Auschwitz with Polish suffering and not the Jewish catastrophe. How is it possible, one can ask, that in a country where the Holocaust was perpetrated, where everybody was aware of the genocide occurring literally in front of them, half of the population believes in pernicious fallacies spun by the authorities? Actually, the phenomenon is not hard to explain, and the memorial techniques are as unsophisticated as they are successful.

First, a handful of undisputed facts: Auschwitz claimed the lives of 1–1.3 million Jews, 70,000–75,000 Poles, 20,000 Roma and 15,000–20,000 people of other nationalities. The Auschwitz complex was an enormous conglomerate of camps, sub-camps and factories all using slave labour, all administered from the original camp, called KL Auschwitz I. This is the site best known today for the rows of red-brick barracks and the iconic sign over the gate which reads *"Arbeit macht frei"* (Work makes you free). This was the place where thousands of Poles, the French, Russians and inmates of many other nationalities worked and died in horrible conditions. Concentration camps (*Konzentrationslager*), including Auschwitz I, were created primarily as places of exploitation, terror and hard labour, where an inmate's death was a by-product of the system, but not its primary objective. Extermination camps (*Vernichtungslager*) had no other purpose than killing. Death was not a by-product – it was the product itself. The death camp Auschwitz II, or Auschwitz-Birkenau, built in 1942, was about 3 kilometres away from the main concentration camp. Unlike prisoners arriving at Auschwitz I, the great majority of Jews brought to Auschwitz II were herded to the undressing rooms and sent straight into the gas chambers. Only the "fortunate" ones, who successfully went through the selection process at the ramp, were given numbers which were tattooed onto their forearms.

In order to create a usable history, to "domesticate" Auschwitz, to make it a part of the Polish national narrative, the accounts of Auschwitz I and Auschwitz II needed to be mixed, blended and confused (as happened in Treblinka) into one universal account of human tragedy. The celebrated Polish author Zofia Nałkowska published the book *Medallions* shortly after the war. Writing about Oświęcim (the Polish name for Auschwitz), she observed: "people prepared this fate for other people". But these "other people" were not selected randomly. They were selected for death because they were Jews. This lesson is easily forgotten today.

In 2006, the Polish Sejm declared 14 June the National Remembrance Day of the Victims of Nazi Concentration Camps. In 2015, the celebration was renamed the National Remembrance Day for Victims of the German-Nazi Concentration and Extermination Camps. These are small changes, but full of meaning. First, the term "Nazi" was found to be no longer adequate in the twenty-first century. Too many people, it was feared, were unable to make an automatic association between the Nazis and the Germans. One had to be more explicit, argued the Polish parliamentarians. Point taken. More importantly, concentration camps, however horrible, were no match – in memorial terms – for the death camps. In the new memorial reality of the European Union, however, the death camps could not be dismissed altogether, as happened in the past. The new commemoration was intended to fill this gap, and deliberately confuse concentration and extermination camps, elevating Polish suffering to the "desired" level of the Holocaust.

The date of the celebration commemorates the first transport of ethnic Poles, political prisoners for the most part, who arrived at Auschwitz I on 14 June 1940. With this transport, Auschwitz finally had the desired stamp of Polish suffering and Polish ethnic and national association. What followed the establishment of the new National Remembrance Day was not difficult to predict. On 14 June 2023, I stood in front of an enormous screen, strategically placed at the Warsaw Central Railway Station, one of the busiest spots in the Polish capital. On the screen were emaciated figures clad in the characteristic striped clothing of concentration camp prisoners. The signs on the screen read: "KL Auschwitz was created to exterminate Poles". The same film was shown over and over, in many other Polish cities. Public spaces and bus shelters were covered with huge posters featuring Auschwitz prisoners. The captions read: "My name is Józef Bałuk. I was 51 when the Germans murdered me in KL Auschwitz because I was a Polish railway worker" and "Poles were the first prisoners of the German death camp in Auschwitz".

Each of these statements was either a bald-faced lie or a half-lie at best. KL Auschwitz was not "created to exterminate the Poles", because the only people exterminated by the Germans at Auschwitz were Jews. Poles were not "the first prisoners of the German death camp in Auschwitz" because they were never sent to the death camp in the first place, and although the Germans did murder many Polish railway workers, they certainly had no policy of killing the Polish members of that particular professional group.

> *"We also were the victims", "The Poles suffered as much as the Jews" ran the headlines*

The Jan Karski Institute of War Losses, which was responsible for this outrageous demonstration of Holocaust negationism, was created in 2022 by the Polish government. Tasked with reinforcing the official state narrative and seeking restitution payments from Germany, it joined the long list of public institutions involved in falsifying the history of the Shoah. The question is, where was the Auschwitz Museum during this whole sordid affair? The Jan Karski Institute's propaganda posters were, after all, based on photographs held in trust by the Auschwitz Museum. During the three-week-long campaign, the history of the camp and its victims was corrupted in front of audiences numbered in the millions. Nevertheless, the Auschwitz Museum, the self-appointed watchdog and gatekeeper of Auschwitz-related information – so active in the media whenever an obscure novel misrepresents the story of the camp – remained oddly silent.

To understand this silence, we need to go back to 2019, when, shortly before the general elections, the Holocaust once again occupied centre stage in Polish political debates. The nationalists were upset about the 2017 US *Justice for Uncompensated Survivors Today Act*, which required the US Department of State to provide a report to Congress on the progress of the restitution of assets seized during or following World War II. The act had no legal relevance for Poland but Polish right-wing zealots viewed it as an opportunity to consolidate their electorate against a common enemy. The message was simple: the Jews are coming back, they want to claim our houses and take our money. The media joined this chorus of indignation: "We also were the victims", "The Poles suffered as much as the Jews" ran the headlines. The exchanges became more and more heated, and the atmosphere filled with antisemitic overtones.

In the middle of the awful campaign of hate, I made a public comment on social media, which, I thought, restated the obvious:

One needs to constantly remind, in Poland, that the German genocidal plan targeted the Jews, and the Jews only, that the extermination camps were for Jews, not for Poles. And that the Polish nation thrives, while the nation of Polish Jews, with its language and tradition, ceased to exist. That's all.

I soon learned that my statement was entirely unacceptable: an organisation called the Institute to Combat Anti-Polonism (funded, generously, by the Polish Ministry of Justice) denounced me to the Prosecutor's Office for slandering the good name of the Polish nation. One could hardly ask for a more egregious example of Holocaust envy.

Incidentally, the Institute to Combat Anti-Polonism is a child of the June 2018 declaration signed jointly by Poland's Mateusz Morawiecki and Israel's Benjamin Netanyahu. Back then, both politicians agreed to place antisemitism and anti-Polonism on equal footing. While antisemitism is an ancient ideology of hate, more recently responsible for 6 million Jewish deaths, anti-Polonism is a strange concept which nowadays exists mostly in the imaginations of Polish nationalists. According to the proponents of this idea, there is a worldwide conspiracy directed against the Polish nation. It is a preposterous notion, and the fact that Israel's PM chose to sign off on such a declaration is just more proof of the desperation of Israeli authorities looking for diplomatic support. Anywhere. It is also another stepping stone on the way to relativising the Holocaust: one of the unstated goals of Holocaust distortionists.

At the same time, the Auschwitz Museum (still considered a reliable and trustworthy source of information by some) published the following statement: "One can assume that more Poles have been killed in Auschwitz II than in Auschwitz I. Birkenau was the largest part of Auschwitz and many prisoners selected in Auschwitz I camp hospital were also murdered in the gas chambers at Birkenau." Can one really assume such a thing? Can we assume that tens of thousands of Poles were delivered to the gas chambers at Birkenau? Really? I very much doubt it. One thing we can assume without any doubt is that during an antisemitic campaign, the Auschwitz Museum declared to the eagerly listening public that the gas chambers of Birkenau could henceforth be considered the centre of Polish suffering.

In 1968, when the communist party started the anti-Jewish campaign, the wrath of the authorities struck an unlikely target: the editors of the Polish scientific encyclopedia. The entry about the concentration camps made a distinction between extermination and concentration camps, indicating that Jews made up 99 per cent of the victims of the former. This was more than the communist authorities could bear. A purge ensued, forty editors lost their jobs, and the new edition of the *Great Scientific*

Encyclopedia no longer differentiated between death camps and concentration camps. Jewish tragedy was once again portrayed as part of the tragedy of the Polish people.

In 2016, this domestication of Auschwitz, and its gradual transformation into a Polish memory site, allowed former prime minister Beata Szydło to deliver – inside the camp – a long speech in which the word "Jew" was pronounced only once: in the context of Poles rescuing Jews. In 2023, Poland's president, Andrzej Duda, delivered a speech in Auschwitz during the annual March of the Living in which he placed on equal footing antisemitism and anti-Polonism. In such a way, Auschwitz has become a name domesticated for the purposes of Polish historical mythology; it has become "usable" history, to employ once again the expression coined by Yehuda Bauer.

> *Auschwitz has become a name domesticated for the purposes of Polish historical mythology*

Creating a usable past

Maria Hochberg-Mariańska was a Jewish writer and journalist who, during the war, was active in a Jewish underground network rescuing Jewish children. Shortly after the war, she found herself in Tarnów: "There was a cabbie, one Staszek, who boasted how he had helped me during the war," Hochberg-Mariańska wrote.

> One day I ran into him and asked him where did these lies come from? He was very surprised: "How come? Don't you remember how many times I saw you in the city, already after the deportations, when there were no more Jews in Tarnów, and I never denounced you to the Germans!" So this was the help which he was boasting so much about.

In fact, Staszek from Tarnów had a point. Helping and abetting the Jews in Poland carried the death penalty. Theoretically, the death penalty could be sought for people who knew about Jews in hiding and failed to inform the authorities. Given that, after 1942, being Jewish was a capital offence, one could speculate that all 24 million ethnic Poles could have, at some point, "rescued" a Jew by failing to denounce the fugitive to the nearest police officer. However ridiculous it may sound to people with even a cursory knowledge of history, this is precisely the argument chosen by the negationist politicians and historians in Poland.

Each year, on 24 March, the Poles celebrate their own virtue. The National Day of Remembrance of Poles Who Rescued Jews Under the German Occupation is an opportunity for politicians to share their thoughts on the rescue efforts undertaken during the war. In his speech on 24 March 2023, President Duda spoke of "one million Poles who gave help to Jews in hiding". Prime Minister Morawiecki went further: "We remember the great Polish history; we remember millions of Poles who suffered and rescued their Jewish neighbours during the cruel night of German occupation. This is the foundation on which we build the great and bright Poland." Jan Żaryn, director of the Roman Dmowski Institute of National Thought, was of a similar opinion, arguing in the European Parliament that there could have been even a million Poles who rescued Jews during the war. It is all nonsense but, as Joseph Goebbels is reputed to have said: "Repeat a lie often enough and it becomes the truth."

The definition of rescue and help is a complex matter. According to Yad Vashem, the Israeli authority responsible for awarding medals to the Righteous Among the Nations, honoured gentiles had to have taken great risks to save Jews during the Holocaust. The forms of help that meet Yad Vashem's criteria include hiding Jews in the rescuer's home or on their property, providing false papers and false identities or smuggling and assisting Jews to escape. Crucially, the rescue activities had to be performed not for financial or other personal gain, but for altruistic reasons. Furthermore, a Jewish testimony was needed to corroborate the noble acts.

Not surprisingly, the verification process and vetting left out many people who, most probably, should have been awarded the medal. Nevertheless, as of 2021, close to 28,000 people from fifty countries have been recognised as Righteous Among the Nations. Poles, who have been awarded 7100 medals, are the largest single national group of the Righteous, followed closely by the Dutch, who hold 5900 medals. Given the size of the Jewish population in pre-war Poland, however, the numbers of Righteous (per capita one person in 3700 received the award) were clearly deemed insufficient by Polish politicians. Year after year dissatisfaction grew in official circles with Yad Vashem's criteria for awarding the coveted medals. Finally, Polish authorities decided to invent their own, more friendly, criteria to expand the ranks of Poles rescuing Jews.

Tadeusz Rydzyk is a Roman Catholic priest of the Redemptorist order and, more importantly, director of Radio Maryja and the TV channel Trwam. In fact, Rydzyk is director of a media/university/business ventures conglomerate at the heart of an ultraconservative, xenophobic and nationalist revolution sweeping the land. In 2017, B'nai B'rith declared that "Radio Maryja has a long history of broadcasting anti-Semitism to its followers", and the US State Department issued a similar warning. During the last several years, however, the antisemitic narrative of Rydzyk's media has been toned down and replaced with gradual, if guarded, appreciation of the politics of Netanyahu-led Israel. Instead of anti-Jewish rants, so frequent in the past, Rydzyk and his media became more and more interested in the Righteous Defence. Jews are nowadays tolerated, or even appreciated, but mostly as objects of charitable acts, true or invented, performed by the altruistic and Catholic Poles during the Holocaust.

Rydzyk's empire includes the John Paul II Museum of Memory and Identity, currently under construction, funded by the Polish taxpayers to the tune of more than US$50 million. According to press releases, the museum will "showcase one thousand years of Christian Poland and John Paul II; it will celebrate Poles who rescued Jews during World War II, and commemorate the 'Cursed Soldiers'". Rydzyk's

This is not the only Pilecki Institute monument backed by dubious historical evidence

efforts have already collected tens of thousands of records of Poles who rescued Jews, and a special Chapel in Memory of Polish Martyrs features 1230 commemorative plaques with names of Poles who were allegedly murdered by the Germans for sheltering Jews. The fact that this is more or less three times as many as the most recent and credible historical research would indicate does not seem to bother Rydzyk, or his sponsors in the government.

The Pilecki Institute, working towards the same goal, created a program, Called by Name. To quote the official Pilecki release:

> The "Called by Name" are Poles who were murdered by the Germans for helping Jews who were at risk of extermination in the Holocaust during the German occupation. The "Called by Name" project aims to do justice to the heroic acts of Poles who consciously risked their own lives and the lives of their loved ones to help Jewish friends, neighbours, and sometimes strangers, and paid the highest price.

The recognition comes in the form of monuments and community events associated with their unveiling. Close to sixty monuments have been unveiled so far; some commemorate Polish Righteous, recognised by Yad Vashem, and some commemorate people like Jadwiga Długoborska. Although there is no credible historical evidence tying Długoborska to saving Jews, she happens to be the aunt of Magdalena Gawin, until recently Poland's deputy minister of culture, and – until April – the director of the Pilecki Institute, which more than compensates for the lack of proof of her noble wartime acts. This is not the only Pilecki monument backed by dubious historical evidence.

What really happened in Markowa

In 2016, the Markowa Ulma-Family Museum of Poles Who Saved Jews in World War II opened for business. Markowa is a village in south-east Poland where the Germans, in March 1944, murdered the Ulmas – a Polish family of eight (parents and children) – and two Jewish families who were hiding in their house. The Ulmas were denounced by their neighbour, a member of the collaborationist auxiliary Polish police. The courage, and ultimate sacrifice, of the Ulma family has been well documented and is at the heart of the museum's exhibition. But the museum is a much more ambitious project. Going beyond the Ulmas, it showcases the rescue efforts of Polish society across the entire Podkarpackie region, a vast area in south-east Poland. It stresses the huge involvement of the Catholic clergy, the brave deeds of the Polish resistance and, of course, the selfless sacrifice of the masses of Polish "bystanders" who saved their Jewish neighbours during the Holocaust. In short, the Ulma museum can be best described as a model of Holocaust distortion, where the courageous acts of the few are shown as the moral choices of the masses.

Holocaust distortion thrives on omission, half-truths and lack of context, leaving us with a deeply flawed historical narrative. Markowa, for instance, was a large village of about 5000 people where the Final Solution to the Jewish Question was executed by the locals, without any Germans present in the area. The concentration and transportation of the local Jews to the nearest German collection point (several kilometres distant) was done by their Polish neighbours. The vast majority of Jews refused to report to the assembly point as ordered, and fled into the nearby woods. That's when the manhunts began. Day after day, week after week, month after month, local Polish firefighters and armed peasants combed the woods looking for the fugitives. Whenever they found any, they robbed them, beat them and delivered them to the Germans for execution. Sometimes the locals raped Jewish women and killed the men without any German assistance. Unsurprisingly, the museum in Markowa has nothing to say about this aspect of Polish–Jewish relations during the war. The museum is there to convey a message of friendship, sacrifice and virtue.

To understand what really happened in Markowa, and why the choices of people like the Ulma family were unique, we need to listen to the voices of the few survivors. Voices that cannot be heard in the museum in Markowa. Jakub Einhorn was one of the Jews of Markowa and the only survivor from his large family. After the war, desperately seeking justice, he testified in a Polish court:

> It happened on December 12, 1942 and I recall this date very vividly, because on December 8, on the previous

Wednesday, they murdered my wife and my child. On that Sunday, when I and my brothers and sisters were hiding at Katarzyna Bar's place, we heard Michał Trznadel, whom we knew well, calling on people at the top of his voice to come to Szmul's house – by which he meant the home of my father, Samuel Einhorn. After some time, I heard the cries of my sisters. I understood that a Jew hunt had begun, so I hid in a chicken coop and that's how I avoided getting caught. From my hideout I could hear, and partially see, what was going on in the yard. I saw clearly my two brothers being led out from the barn of Wojciech Krauze, our neighbour. They were dragged out from the barn by Krauze and Orzechowski (the son-in-law of the Markowa blacksmith). There were some other men too, but I do not recall their names anymore. I saw that one of my brothers was bleeding, and that blood trickled down his face; I also heard that Orzechowski and Krauze wounded my brother while they gave him a beating inside the barn. I heard how Antoni Bar reproached Krauze: "Why do you beat him up, is it not enough that you take him for execution? ... The Zeligs were caught by Andrzej Rewer, Michał Szpytma and other firefighters. Andrzej Rewer kept watch the whole night over the cellar in which the Jews had been placed. Franciszek Bar told me that Rewer offered the village elder to leave the

Gestapo alone and that he – Rewer – would kill the Jews himself, if they only paid him 50 zlotys per head. The next day, as I heard from Michał Drewniak, Rewer tied up the captives and brought them out to the field, where the police already waited and where all these Jews were shot. I know for a fact that the Firefighting Brigade and the men from the village took part in the manhunt.

If we are to believe Mateusz Szpytma (a native of Markowa, and today deputy director of the IPN), who curated the Markowa museum exhibition, Jakub Einhorn must have simply misunderstood the whole situation. It was only the Germans, he writes, who hunted down the Jews in Markowa. One of their victims – Szpytma tells us, in a book he co-wrote about the Ulma family – as he was being led to his execution, cried out to his Polish neighbour: "Farewell, my friend!" So much for Szpytma. Let's instead hear more from the Jewish survivors. Mosze Weltz was hiding close to Markowa. After the war, he wrote in testimony presented to the Central Jewish Historical Commission in 1947:

> [D]uring the *Aktion* in Sieniawa, some of the Jews escaped, some hid in the bunkers. The Poles knew about it and they organised, on their own, a hunt for the Jews, in order to rob

them and to murder them. In Markowa, a village close to Łańcut, the Poles found twenty-eight Jews and they killed them. They took everything, they even pulled out golden teeth from their victims. Antoni Cyran was the leader of the posse. He took over the Jewish real estate and today, he still lives in the same village. In Markowa, there is a grave where two hundred Jews from that area were buried, all shot by the Poles.

Yehuda Ehrlich, another survivor, was hiding in Sietesz, a nearby village located just beyond a small hill, less than 2 kilometres east of the last houses of Markowa. Ehrlich's testimony, now in the Yad Vashem archive, is poignant and to the point:

> These were hard times for them [Jan and Maria Wiglusz, his gentile hosts] and for us. Searches were conducted both by the Germans and by the Polish peasants themselves, who wanted to find the hidden Jews. In the spring of 1944 a Jewish family was discovered hiding with Polish peasants. The Polish family – eight souls, including a pregnant wife – was killed with the hidden Jews. As a result, there was enormous panic among the Polish peasants who were hiding the Jews. The next morning twenty-four corpses of Jews were discovered in the fields. They had been murdered

by the peasants themselves, peasants who had kept them hidden during [the previous] twenty months.

In light of these testimonies the issue of rescuing the Jews in Markowa (and elsewhere in the region) acquires a very different meaning. Hiding Jews was, no doubt, the most dangerous of all kinds of underground resistance activities. But the real threat was not the Germans – stationed in Przeworsk or Łańcut, miles away and largely clueless as to the whereabouts of the Jews – but one's own neighbours, who took part in manhunts or were ready to denounce rescuers to the authorities. In Poland, during the war, hiding Jews was so dangerous precisely because there was no social permission to engage in it. This essential part of the historical context is sadly missing from the Markowa museum. None of these Jewish voices can be heard there. What we see in Markowa is no longer an account of history but the myth of Righteous Defence deployed to safeguard the historical innocence of the nation.

The Markowa museum is not a stand-alone operation; it is part of a larger memorial offensive. The Museum of Martyrdom of Polish Villages opened with great fanfare in 2021 in Michniów, a small village 160 kilometres south of Warsaw, close to Kielce. Michniów was razed by the Germans on 12–13 July 1943. Two hundred local inhabitants were summarily executed there for assisting the partisans. The new museum commemorates not only the tragedy of Michniów, but also the sacrifice of all Polish villagers during World War II. The main exhibition tells the story of Polish peasants suffering under the Soviet and German occupations. Outside the museum, rows of crosses stand guard over huge boulders, each representing a Polish village destroyed by either the Germans or the Ukrainian nationalists. The idea has obviously been lifted from Treblinka, where similar boulders represent the annihilated Jewish communities. Before leaving the museum, visitors transit through a dark corridor, which holds an exhibition about Polish peasants rescuing Jews. This exhibition is a copy of the Markowa museum exhibition. There are the Righteous Poles with medals, the Jews grateful for their rescue, and the German reprisals. In short, the Righteous Defence in its pure form. The museum, which (to believe its name) should cover the martyrdom of Polish villages, is one more sweet, patriotic, myth-based account of Polish innocence during the war.

> *The museum is one more sweet, patriotic, myth-based account of Polish innocence during the war*

In the Michniów museum, one would look in vain for a mention of Jewish life in the Polish villages – and rural Jewish society in the Kielce region was a truly noteworthy phenomenon. The roundups of Jews in the villages and their transfer to the nearest ghettos were repeated, during the 1940–42 period, hundreds of times across the occupied land. Sadly, there is not even a word about it in the museum. Bodzentyn, where twelve-year-old Dawid Rubinowicz wrote his diary (later translated and published in English) before being taken to Treblinka, is just 10 kilometres from the museum.

> 12 August [1940]: All through the war I have been studying at home by myself. When I think of how I used to go to school I feel like bursting into tears, and today I must stay at home and can't go anywhere.
>
> September 1 [1940]: I remember what we've already gone through in this short time, how much suffering we've already experienced.
>
> May 6 [1942]: Papa! – Papa, where are you? If only I could see you once more ... And then I saw him on the last lorry; his eyes were red with weeping. I kept on looking at him until he disappeared around the corner, then I had a sudden fit of crying, and I felt how much I love him and how much he loves me ...

In the Michniów museum not even a word about little Dawid, his life and death. During the liquidation actions, in the summer and autumn of 1942, Polish villages saw thousands of Jews marched to death transports – still nothing. And then the manhunts, the burnings of houses where Jews found refuge. Nothing. A large forest starts right behind the Michniów museum. It is here, less than 2 kilometres away from the impressive building, that – in August 1944 – the White Colours unit of Home Army partisans murdered fifty Jews – children, women and men, refugees from the HASAG factory in Skarżysko-Kamienna. In the museum – not a word about it. This is a museum of *Polish* suffering, full stop, end of story.

The Holocaust is not a part of our history

In the spring of 2013, I met with Bogdan Zdrojewski, then Poland's minister of culture. We talked about the soon-to-be-opened Museum of the History of Polish Jews and about the place of the Holocaust in Polish history. Our opinions on this topic differed. Later on, I met with Małgorzata Omilanowska, Zdrojewski's deputy (soon to become his successor), a respected art historian. Visibly agitated, Omilanowska complained about the sites of death camps, which had become such a "memorial hot potato" for the Polish state and the Polish people. "It is a poisoned pill, a cuckoo's egg, left behind by the Germans that we now have to maintain, to pay for, to be responsible for!" exclaimed the deputy minister of culture.

For her, as for so many other people in Poland, death camps had nothing to do with their history, and definitely had no relation to Polish society. As alien artefacts, these spaces were something without any link to, and relevance for, the national past. It was a German and Jewish thing, the minister hinted darkly. My attempts to argue that 3 million Jews murdered in the Holocaust, in these camps, were Polish citizens – that this alone made it a crucial part of Polish history – were dismissed as irrelevant. The issue of Polish complicity in the implementation of the Final Solution, the scale of theft of Jewish property, the thousands of well-documented murders of Jews at the hands of the Poles, the deadly efficiency of Polish collaborationist police, the enormous scale of denunciations – all these difficult questions were taboo back in 2013, and they continue to be taboo today.

This disassociation from the event takes truly bizarre forms. Polish state museums, like all state institutions in Poland, have an internet domain ending with the letters "pl". There is one exception: the museums attached to the former death camps have generic "eu" or "org" domains: Majdanek.eu, Sobibor-memorial.eu, Belzec.eu, Muzeumtreblinka.eu, and Auschwitz.org. Poland has nothing to do with the camps, we are being told. It goes further. In 1939, soon after the conquest of Poland, the Germans rebaptised Łódź, the second-largest Polish city, as Litzmannstadt, to honour Karl Litzmann, a World War I general and Nazi politician. They also established in Łódź the second-largest ghetto, prison to 200,000 Jews. Today, the authorities insist on calling the Łódź Ghetto the Litzmannstadt Ghetto, perpetuating the Nazi nomenclature. There is more. Płaszów is a neighborhood in Cracow, where Germans organised the notorious concentration camp portrayed in the film *Schindler's List*. Today, the camp museum has lost its Polish diacritics and is officially known as the Plaszow Museum. Given the number of German-imposed toponyms in occupied Poland, one can only wonder when the official narrative will start to refer to the Warsaw Ghetto as Warschauer Ghetto, or to the ghetto in Rzeszów as Ghetto Reichshof, as Rzeszów was known back then.

> *The only time the Jewish catastrophe enters the curriculum is when the righteous rescuers need to be mentioned*

The Polish Historical Association (or PTH) is the largest and oldest professional association of historians in Poland. The PTH holds its general meetings every five years. Over the past thirty years, PTH members have delivered hundreds of papers at these meetings and organised hundreds of panel discussions. They considered the state of research dealing with all periods of Polish history, from the Middle Ages until today. The only event that somehow escaped the scrutiny of Polish historians was the

Holocaust, arguably the greatest tragedy in Polish history. It is, *toutes proportions gardées*, as if among the thousands of papers presented at the annual meetings of the American Historical Association over the past three decades, not one addressed the issue of North American slavery or the destruction of Native American societies. The Holocaust has been so successfully purged from Polish history that its absence does not bother even the people who ought to keep the record – Polish historians. The only time the Jewish catastrophe enters the curriculum is when the righteous rescuers need to be mentioned.

In April 2015, James Comey, then head of the FBI, visited the exhibition "Some Were Neighbors" at the United States Holocaust Memorial Museum in Washington, D.C. This important exhibition dealt with the involvement of gentiles in the tragedy of their Jewish neighbours, an often understudied aspect of the history of the Holocaust. Before leaving the museum, Comey gave an important and moving speech:

> Good people helped murder millions. And that's the most frightening lesson of all – that our very humanity made us capable of, even susceptible to, surrendering our individual moral authority to the group, where it can be hijacked by evil. Of being so cowed by those in power. Of convincing ourselves of nearly anything. In their minds,

the murderers and accomplices of Germany, and Poland, and Hungary, and so many, many other places didn't do something evil. They convinced themselves it was the right thing to do, the thing they had to do. That's what people do. And that should truly frighten us.

No one could say it better than the most important law enforcement officer in the United States.

Comey put his finger on one of the essential problems, which baffled scholars of the genocide: the apparent ease with which millions of people were seduced by an ideology of hate and fear, and encouraged to act in an inhuman way. This paradigm of hate is not specific to the Holocaust; it applies equally to the genocides in Rwanda, Bosnia, Cambodia or any other unfortunate place where a group of people happened to have been slated for death due to their nationality, religion or race. In short, the director of the FBI brought to our attention an issue of universal importance.

In Poland, the reaction to Comey's speech was immediate, and furious. President Bronisław Komorowski, Prime Minister Ewa Kopacz and the speaker of the parliament, Radosław Sikorski, all requested that Comey apologise to Poland and to Polish society. It was the association with Germans that drove the moral outrage of Polish politicians. Cries of "We were victims, not the culprits" and "Millions of Poles died during the war" resonated once again in political speeches and in the media. All of this happened while Poland was still a democratic country, several months before the Polish nationalists came to power.

A few days later, the directors of the largest Polish museums decided to join the chorus of moral indignation, and penned their own letter to Comey. It read as follows:

> Dear Mr. Comey, we are deeply concerned about the words you have said in the United States Holocaust Memorial Museum. For the sake of better understanding of Polish, Jewish and world history of the 20th century, we would like to invite you to pay a visit to Poland. As the heads of our country's most important museums and educational institutions dealing with the history of the period, we would like to offer you a study visit which will allow you not only to get to know, but also to understand in a more complete way the twists and turns of history of the occupied Europe. This, in the future, could prevent you from making mistakes leading to negative repercussions in the friendly relations between our countries and peoples.

What are the errors that the directors of Polish memorial museums referred to? What was Comey supposed to learn during the "study visit" offered to him? If a visit to the Auschwitz Museum or the POLIN Museum were to convince the director of the FBI that the Holocaust was purely a German affair, that other nations had nothing to do with the tragedy, that there were no Polish murderers of Jews – this would mean that Polish memorial museums were lying about the past and grossly falsifying the history of the Holocaust.

Comey was absolutely right: the tragedy of the Jews during the Holocaust was in part caused by ordinary people who became willing participants in the German genocidal plan. Polish historians who study Jewish testimonies and post-war trial records readily recognise the grim picture of moral corruption which touched the "good" people who, during the occupation, became executioners of their neighbours. Comey could have extended the list of culprits further, adding to it the French, Belgians, Dutch, Ukrainians, Belorussians and Balts. But does their absence take anything away from the validity of his argument? I don't think so. Harming Jews, or preying on Jewish misery, became a widespread phenomenon during the Holocaust, occurring – albeit to varying degrees – in all countries of occupied Europe.

> *"You know very well that the Polish nation did not participate in the Holocaust"*

The letter was signed (this came as no surprise) by the directors of the IPN, the Polish History Museum, the Warsaw Uprising Museum and the World War II Museum. The fact that Piotr Cywiński, the director of the Auschwitz Museum, and Dariusz Stola, the director of the Museum of the History of Polish Jews – who had a special responsibility as custodians of memory of the Jewish victims and must have known that the head of the FBI was right – signed the letter was not only a scandal, but also – more importantly – a warning, a grim harbinger of the brown wave, which in the coming months and years was to overflow the dams and spill all over Poland. It was precisely these kinds of voices that legitimised the far right, which for years had marched under the banner of Polish innocence.

At the time when the directors of Polish memorial museums wrote their letter, millions of Poles watched the all-important presidential televised debate. Andrzej Duda, the young and energetic candidate of the Polish nationalists, asked the incumbent president Komorowski the following question:

> In 2011, at the ceremony commemorating the victims in Jedwabne, you sent a letter … In it you included the statement: "the nation of the victims was also a perpetrator". Mr President, what is your policy of defending Poland's good name if you use a term in your speeches that destroys

real historical memory? It is so very important to us, not to be falsely accused by the others of having taken part in the Holocaust. You know very well that the Polish nation did not participate in the Holocaust.

The candidate of the Polish right was using precisely the same language and logic as the directors of Polish memorial museums: refusing, against all available evidence, to acknowledge any association of Polish society with the Holocaust. In the end, the message of the nationalist contender carried the day and Duda won the presidency. Can one say with certainty that playing the antisemitic card did not contribute to the electoral victory of Poland's current president? The question asked during the presidential debate was, after all, based on a denial of the history of the Holocaust. Is there any other country on Earth where such a declaration would be possible in a presidential debate, or even imaginable?

The fact that in the second decade of the twenty-first century, eighty years after the event, three generations after the nation of Polish Jews was wiped off the face of the earth, Polish politicians could still raise their electoral prospects riding the wave of antisemitic feelings is a testimony to the power and the longevity of Holocaust denial, today better known as Holocaust distortion, or negationism.

What can be done?

For many years scholars and teachers discussed the future of Holocaust education and its commemoration. The debates revolved around the inevitable passing of the generation of Holocaust survivors. What kind of challenges would we face once the witnesses of the genocide were no longer with us? Who would tell the story; who would say "I was there, I saw it, it happened to me"? Some believed that digitisation of historical records was the answer, others went looking for the last Jewish witnesses, who had not yet been heard from, and still others turned to the promises of modern technology, working on interactive two- and three-dimensional displays, hoping to attract the attention of the younger generation. The main concern was the threat of a growing indifference towards an event that was more and more distant.

Today, we know that indifference to the Holocaust is no longer an issue. The true challenge, one for which most of us were unprepared, is Holocaust distortion. The interest in the history and in the commemoration of the Shoah is nowadays greater than ever. Unfortunately, more and more often this is for all the wrong reasons. Fed by a toxic mix of lies and half-truths, and fuelled by the enormous resources of the state, the memory of the Shoah is being hijacked by people and institutions wishing to transform the past into something usable, into a past which can not only be reconciled with the tales of their own innocence, but can also reinforce these myths. Holocaust denial, built on simple lies (which could never challenge our understanding of the Shoah), has now been replaced by a much more dangerous and insidious foe.

The assault on the history of the Holocaust needs to be seen as part of a larger assault on the tenets of democratic society. It's needed to stir the nationalistic sense of belonging, to build up the idea of *Volksgemeinschaft*, and to undermine democratic institutions. In Poland, Holocaust distortion, or negationism, has become part of an ambitious political project which has gradually, step by step, attempted to move the country towards a fascist form of government. Joanna Tokarska-Bakir, one of Poland's leading cultural anthropologists and historians, identified the approaching danger:

> It is fascism understood not at all as an insult, but as an analytical concept, describing a specific type of ruling the masses. It is characterised by authoritarianism ... A drive to subjugate the opposition and create absolute ideological domination. A crucial role in the debate, facilitated by the seizure of public media, is played by political fact-bending, which dominates any substantive discussion. In the event that the existing elites do not support the point of view

of the authorities, their own elites are called in. The ultimate argument in establishing the truth of the facts is the claim of the nation as the ultimate source of political order. Moreover, the system invokes a specifically formatted patriotism that stigmatises as treason any criticism of the state, especially abroad.

The interview, which was published in 2016, appeared under the headline: "The Butcher on the Horizon". During the next several years the butcher entered Polish living rooms.

The negationists don't hesitate to employ the language of hate perfected in the 1930s and 1940s. Antisemitic tropes are used against "the others", in order to consolidate the electorate with the help of an invented threat. The Jews, as it has been shown, can become targets of attack but, most often, it is people of colour, migrants from the south or members of sexual minorities who find themselves at the centre of campaigns orchestrated by the negationists. The tools of hate, however, remain the same. In 2015, shortly before the general elections, Jarosław Kaczyński, leader of the right-wing, nationalistic Law and Justice Party, gave a speech in which he referred to the migrants reaching Europe in large numbers: "We already see cases of very dangerous diseases, long forgotten in Europe. Cholera in Greece, dysentery in Vienna, various kinds of parasites and protozoans, which can be harmless in the organisms of these people, but which can be dangerous for us."

Awful and primitive propaganda by any standard, Kaczyński's words played on familiar anti-Jewish tropes, easily understood by Polish audiences. *Jews, Lice, Typhus* was the title of a Polish-language film directed by Herbert Gerdes that played in all Polish cinemas in 1941 and 1942. The campaign of hate, associating Jews with the deadly disease, was planned by German propagandists and deployed in Poland, and involved newsreels, posters, travelling exhibitions, newspaper articles and leaflets distributed with ration cards. The message reached practically everyone across the occupied land. Testimonies from Jewish survivors illustrate how effective it was during the war, and later became an integral part of the popular antisemitic imaginarium. Kaczyński's choice of words was not accidental: the message struck a familiar chord and played into Poland's darkest and most primitive fears. Using similar techniques, the nationalist and negationist politicians targeted sexual minorities.

Holocaust distortion and negationism go hand in hand with the growing authoritarian and populist assault on democracy

In 2020, during the most recent presidential campaign, Andrzej Duda, the incumbent president, declared at a public rally: "They want to tell us that LGBT are people, but it is just an ideology." Przemysław Czarnek, then a member of Duda's electoral campaign staff, now an MP and former minister of education, went a step further: "We have to defend ourselves against the LGBT ideology, we will no longer listen to this nonsense about some kind of human rights and some kind of equality. These people are not equal to normal people and let's finally end this discussion." The echoes of the past are unmistakable. Stripping away human characteristics from your opponents has been at the core of every fascist textbook of the recent past.

Holocaust distortion and negationism are today on the rise, and they go hand in hand with the growing authoritarian and populist assault on democracy. What can be done? On 10 September 2023 the church and state officials held a ceremony to celebrate the beatification of the Ulma family by the Catholic church. It was a huge celebration, featuring a 700-strong choir and an orchestra made up of 500 musicians. President Duda and then prime minister Morawiecki graced the ceremonies with their presence. Should the Ulmas be commemorated? Yes, of course. Should they be commemorated now? Absolutely not. In the present context of militant nationalism, of Holocaust denial and distortion, the ultimate sacrifice of the Ulma family is being cynically used by people in bad faith and presented as the default position of Polish society during the war.

The moment to celebrate the Ulmas, and all the other Polish Righteous, will only come when Polish society, and the Polish state, is ready to also commemorate Jews who have been murdered by Poles. In Markowa, one needs first to commemorate the Tencer family, the Zelig family, Jakub Einhorn's wife, daughter, brothers and sisters; let us remember Tauba Szpechl, Ksyl Hirszfeld and so many anonymous Jewish victims, all of whom were either murdered or delivered to the Germans by their Polish neighbours in the same village where the Ulmas met their end. Then, and only then, can we commemorate, with clear conscience, the tragedy of the Ulma family, or any other Polish family who sacrificed their lives trying to save their Jewish neighbours.

What can be done about the sites of Jewish catastrophe which today are being progressively taken over by the memorial excesses of the Polish state? Can we allow the sites where millions of Jews have been put to death to become monuments of Polish martyrdom? Perhaps the time has come to declare Treblinka, Auschwitz, Bełżec, Sobibor and Chełmno sites of tragic heritage for humanity as a whole. Perhaps the renaming of the internet domains of death camp museums has been, after all (and despite the original intent), a step in the right direction? Given the apparent unwillingness of the Polish authorities to act as honest custodians of the memory of the Holocaust, perhaps the time has come to place these sites under European, United Nations or other international jurisdictions. Exterritorial, like embassies, Auschwitz and Treblinka could become places in which humanity can reflect unhindered on one of the greatest catastrophes in history, on its own tragic heritage, and its own moral condition, past and present. ≡

Past issues

"For a long time now, the authority of knowledge has been under siege from those who march under the banner of pure belief."
—Simon Schama

The Return of History investigates rising global populism, and the forces propelling modern nativism and xenophobia.

"Traditional principles and allegiances have given way to realpolitik." —Lina Khatib

The New Middle East examines the dramatic changes unfolding in the region as new rivalries, blocs and partnerships are formed – based not on ideology but on pragmatism.

"The left has become the ideology that dare not speak its name." —Anshel Pfeffer

In *The Strange Death and Curious Rebirth of the Israeli Left*, Anshel Pfeffer takes the pulse of Israel's left wing, examining its health and prospects and dissecting the country's complex post-Netanyahu political reality.

"If ink on paper can reassemble a world …"
—Rachel Kadish

The Jewish world of pre-war Europe was almost destroyed. If we hold up a lantern to that darkness, what can we discover about what was lost, what survived and what could have been?

"Younger writers were freed to think about specifically Jewish questions. [Their] work has a narrower appeal. Only time will tell if it is also a deeper one." —Adam Kirsch

After the Golden Age examines the current generation of leading American Jewish writers as they grapple with questions about religion, Israel, politics and multiculturalism.

"Iran's strategy is to eat away at American power, while legitimising its own role as a regional power with nuclear ambitions."
—Kim Ghattas

Iran examines the motivations behind the country's changing role and influence in the Middle East, delving into the regime's secretive strategy and tactics.

"The process of saying goodbye to these two authors, who had been a visible presence in Israeli society for decades, is far from over."
—Nir Baram

The Pen and the Sword explores the efforts by successive generations of Israeli writers to grapple with their nation's difficult political questions.

"Ukrainians voted for a mixture of Benny Hill and Boris Johnson, and they somehow wound up with Churchill."
—Vladislav Davidzon

The Jews of Ukraine explores the rich, tumultuous history of the Jews of Ukraine, who have played a pivotal role in modern Jewish life.

"I need to understand what no one yet understands: why, after nearly thirty years, there has been no justice." —Javier Sinay

The AMIA Bombing delves into the unresolved questions and political intrigue surrounding the terrorist attack that destroyed Buenos Aires' Jewish community centre in 1994.

"Our religion, our story, is, at its heart, a love of this language and a refusal to let it go."
—Ben Judah

Ivrit explores the remarkable evolution and revival of Hebrew – a language whose trajectory charts the recent history of the Jewish people.

"Though he is already preparing to send astronauts to the moon, Musk has been consistently underestimated, and now the danger he presents is being underestimated as well."
—Richard Cooke

Dark Star explores the troubling political devolution of Elon Musk.

"October 7 was horrific. Then came October 8, and that's when Jews understood how hated they really are."
—Hadley Freeman

Blindness explores the willingness of progressives to abandon values they purport to represent.

Add these past issues to your subscription when buying online.

Subscribe to The Jewish Quarterly and save.

Enjoy free delivery of The Jewish Quarterly to your door, digital access to every issue of The Jewish Quarterly for one year, and exclusive special offers.

Forthcoming issue:

JQ258: The Rudashevski Diary

(November 2024)

Never miss an issue.
Subscribe and save.

- 1 year* print and digital subscription (4 issues) £55 GBP | $75 USD
- 1 year* digital subscription (4 issues) £35 GBP | $45 USD

Subscribe now:

Visit jewishquarterly.com/subscribe

Email subscribe@jewishquarterly.com

Scan one of these QR codes with your mobile device camera app:

Subscribe in £GBP   Subscribe in $USD

PRICES INCLUDE POSTAGE AND HANDLING.
Prices and discounts current at the time of printing. We also offer subscriptions in AUD for subscribers from Australia, New Zealand and Asia, and for existing subscribers to Schwartz Media titles. See our website for more information. *Your subscription will automatically renew until you notify us to stop. We will send you a reminder notice prior to the end of your subscription period.